ETERNITY, TIME, AND
THE LIFE OF WISDOM

Faith and Reason: Studies in Catholic Theology and Philosophy

The series aims at publishing scholarly studies that serve the project of "faith seeking understanding." We hope to assist in making available in English valuable work being done by theologians and philosophers abroad; in this regard we recognize a special place for the ongoing renaissance in French-language Thomistic theology and philosophy. In addition to translations, we intend to publish collections of essays and monographs from a range of perspectives, united by their common commitment to the ecclesial and sapiential work of "faith seeking understanding" so as to build up the Church and proclaim the Gospel afresh.

Co-editors

Michael Dauphinais, *Ave Maria University*
Reinhard Hütter, *Duke University Divinity School*
Matthew Levering, *Ave Maria University*

Advisory Board

Romanus Cessario, OP, *St. John's Seminary*
Gilles Emery, OP, *University of Fribourg*
Joseph Koterski, SJ, *Fordham University*
Matthew L. Lamb, *Ave Maria University*
Steven A. Long, *Ave Maria University*
Guy Mansini, OSB, *Saint Meinrad Seminary*
Bruce Marshall, *Southern Methodist University*
Charles Morerod, OP, *Angelicum*
Francesca Aran Murphy, *University of Aberdeen*
John O'Callaghan, *University of Notre Dame*
R. R. Reno, *Creighton University*
Richard Schenk, OP, *Dominican School of Philosophy and Theology*

Published Volumes

Gilles Emery, OP, *Trinity, Church, and the Human Person: Thomistic Essays*
Matthew L. Lamb, *Eternity, Time, and the Life of Wisdom*

Future Volumes

Serge-Thomas Bonino, OP, ed., *Surnaturel: Reflections on Nature and Grace*
Guy Mansini, OSB, *Christology and Ecclesiology*

ETERNITY, TIME, AND THE LIFE OF WISDOM

Matthew L. Lamb

Sapientia Press
of Ave Maria University

Requests for permission to make copies of any part of the work should be directed to:

Sapientia Press
of Ave Maria University
1025 Commons Circle
Naples, FL 34119
888-343-8607

Cover Design: Eloise Anagnost

Cover Image: Detail from a plaque with the Journey to Emmaus and the Noli Me Tangere. ca. 1115–1120. Ivory, traces of gilding, $10\,^5/8 \times 5\,^5/16$ in. (27×13.5 cm). Spanish, made in León. Gift of J. Pierpont Morgan, 1917 (17.190.47). The Metropolitan Museum of Art, New York, NY, U.S.A. A complete view of the plaque appears on page 162.

Cover image copyright © The Metropolitan Museum of Art/Art Resource, NY

Printed in the United States of America.

Library of Congress Control Number: 2007928729

ISBN-10: 1-932589-41-4

ISBN-13: 978-1-932589-41-2

Table of Contents

Preface

BIRTHDAYS are celebrations of the gifts we are and have received: our life, our family, our friends. Most of all they should be celebrations of the gratitude we render to the Triune God from whom, in whom, and to whom we live and move and have our being. I am grateful to my colleagues and friends, Matthew Levering and Michael Dauphinais, for assembling these essays and, more importantly, for all their own excellent theological publications, teaching, and tireless labor for the renewal of Catholic intellectual and theological life.

At a young age I joined a contemplative monastic community where I was blessed with wise spiritual and intellectual guidance. Studying the Fathers of the Church along with the great monastic theologians opened my mind and heart to the reality of Jesus Christ, the risen Lord of all that is, and his revelation of the Father in the Holy Spirit. The rhythm of this "lectio divina" with the Divine Office and the Holy Sacrifice of the Mass deepens one's realization of the Triune Presence of Father, Son, and Holy Spirit. The light of charity informed faith in no way darkened or narrowed the light of intelligence and reason. Quite the contrary. Faith enlightened, healed, and intensified the light of reason. I came to appreciate why, during the first millennium of Christianity, it was in the patristic and monastic communities, with their dedication to holiness and wisdom, that the great classics of East and West were preserved and cherished.

The monastic, convent, and cathedral schools and libraries, rooted in the quest for wisdom and holiness, enabled the development in Europe of universities where intellectual life would be further developed under the aegis of a quest for science and scholarship. The Dominicans and Franciscans sought to assure that science and scholarship would not be severed from attention to wisdom and holiness. In reading St. Thomas Aquinas and St. Bonaventure one encounters a wonderful communion of the infused holy wisdom as gift of the Holy Spirit with the acquired contemplative or speculative metaphysical "scientia" attuning minds and hearts to the ordered whole of creation and redemption. As the second millennium of Christianity came to an end, it was all too clear that empirical science and scholarship had been drastically severed from wisdom and holiness. An ideology of progress robbed the great classics of philosophy and theology of their truth, relegating their study to a historicist relativism as if they were fit only for museum reliquaries of long dead minds. My monastic vocation engendered a realization that the great wars and horrors of the twentieth century risked extinguishing the light of reason in a terrifying nihilism. The light of faith was needed to rescue human intelligence and cultures from what St. Augustine calls "the disordered desire for domination" *(libido dominandi).*

During the last sessions of the Second Vatican Council I was sent to Rome to study and obtain an STL at the Pontifical Gregorian University. There I studied principally with Professor Bernard Lonergan, SJ, whose writings on Aquinas had introduced me to the intellectual asceticism needed to appreciate the speculative achievements of the Angelic Doctor. His guidance enabled me to appreciate the intellectual and moral dimensions of St. Augustine's conversion to Christ, and how Aquinas transposed Augustine's narrative into his own treatment of how the theological virtues related to the intellectual and moral virtues. In conversations and writings Fr. Lonergan spoke of the derailment of intelligence through nominalism and voluntarism, of the longer cycle of decline that was exacerbated by the European Enlightenment with its rejection of wisdom and the subordination of science to technologies of power. His attention to the interiority of the human spirit, to the practice of contemplative "theoria" in his retrieval and transposition of Aquinas's cognitional theory (what do we do when we know?) indicated ways of transforming post-Enlightenment cultures by informing them with the Catholic truth and wisdom of the biblical, patristic, and scholastic traditions.

As a Canadian Fr. Lonergan called my attention to the achievements of the generations of Catholic immigrants in the United States, how they had developed educational and health care institutions on such a vast scale. I began to realize the importance of Catholic higher education if these two pillars of the Enlightenment (education and health care) were to be informed with a wisdom and holiness that could counteract the secularist tendencies toward dehumanizing scientism and nihilistic relativism. Having witnessed the ways that the mass media coverage of Vatican II had distorted the import of the Council into progressive liberals versus reactionary conservatives, thereby seducing many Catholic intellectuals into minimizing the true achievements of the tradition, Fr. Lonergan recommended that I do doctoral work in Germany where Catholic theology faculty had more experience dealing with secularist tendencies in the state universities of which they were a part. The first German work he recommended me to read was Hans Urs von Balthasar's *Die Wahrheit der Welt*. The truth of the world requires attentiveness to both gifted and acquired wisdom and knowledge.

A short stay in Tübingen provided the opportunity to speak with then Professor Joseph Ratzinger about his work on Augustine just before he left for Regensburg, with Professor Max Seckler about Aquinas, and to gauge the gathering winds of controversy in the historicist positions advocated by Professor Hans Küng. I went on to the State University of Münster in Westfalen where, thanks to the recommendation of Professor Johann Baptist Metz, I had a government scholarship to pursue doctoral studies with him in the Catholic faculty of theology. Emeritus Professor Josef Pieper occasionally held brilliant lectures on Aquinas. I was not attracted to a historical study of Aquinas—fifteen years of studying the Fathers and Aquinas had convinced me of the truth of their achievements, as they baptized the philosophical wisdom of the Greeks and Romans with the light of faith and friendship with Jesus Christ. If the Catholic intellectual apostolate was to begin the task of evangelizing contemporary cultures in line with the invitation of Vatican II, one had to show where the abandonment of faith and wisdom had led, not to the liberation and flourishing of human life, but to its degradation. Without this dialectic of the ancient and medievals vis-à-vis the moderns the needed historical retrieval of the Fathers and Schoolmen could lose its transcultural truth and be relegated in the academy to mere historicism.

Fr. Metz's willingness to confront this, even and especially in the horrors of his own Germany and the Holocaust, was most helpful in this task. He rejected the facile media portrayal of post-Vatican II Catholicism as engaged in a superficial struggle of conservatives and liberals. In one of our early conversations he directed my attention to Benedict Spinoza's *Theologico-Political Treatise* as laying the foundations for a modern historical-criticism that is thoroughly historicist and relativist: The Bible is only a collection of texts, the meaning of any text can only be with reference to another text, and above all the question of the truth of the realities revealed must be rigorously excluded. The recovery and transposition of the political theological problem in contemporary cultures indicates that religious truth must be approached in the context of wisdom rather than dominative power.

In the context of Fr. Metz's project to bring theology as a sapiential science into interdisciplinary collaboration with the human and natural sciences, I did a doctoral dissertation comparing and contrasting Wilhelm Dilthey's critique of historical reason and what I termed Bernard Lonergan's meta-method. In Germany, thanks to the thorough scholarship of Professor Giovanni Sala, SJ, on Immanuel Kant and Bernard Lonergan, it was clear that Lonergan's method was not "transcendental" in any Kantian sense. Fr. Metz was also interested in the ways that Fr. Lonergan's work differed from that of his friend and mentor, Fr. Karl Rahner, SJ. My dissertation indicated that Lonergan's approach situates the question of truth within the wisdom contexts of metaphysics and theology, whereas Dilthey's approach never overcame, despite his efforts, a relativist historicism.

A decade of teaching at Marquette University and two decades at Boston College have provided me with a real appreciation of the massive and long-term efforts required in a genuinely Catholic intellectual apostolate to evangelize American culture. Dangers abound, both personal and institutional, to internalize and rationalize the disorders of the age rather than keeping alive the wisdom of the Cross. My own failings, as well as those of so many Catholic schools, colleges, and universities, are manifold and in need of correction, forgiveness, and renewed dedication to the Catholic intellectual apostolate. Cardinal Newman stated the issue forcefully in his famous *Bigleitto Speech*:

> Liberalism in religion is the doctrine that there is no positive truth in religion, but that one creed is as good as another, and this is the teaching which is gaining substance and force daily. It is inconsistent with any recognition of any religion as true. It teaches that all are to be tolerated, for all are matters of opinion. Revealed religion is not a

truth, but a sentiment and a taste; not an objective fact, not miraculous; and it is the right of each individual to make it say just what strikes his fancy.

Newman's stated forcefully that for "thirty, forty, fifty years I have resisted to the best of my powers the spirit of Liberalism in religion. Never did Holy Church need champions against it more sorely than now, when, alas!, it is an error overspreading, as a snare, the whole earth. . . ." This is still our task. To enlighten post-Enlightenment cultures with the light of revealed truth and metaphysical wisdom, as Pope John Paul II and Pope Benedict XVI teach, is a major challenge facing Catholic higher education.

At the beginning of the third millennium of Christianity Ave Maria University is dedicated, in collaboration with many around the world, to integrating science, scholarship, and the arts with the perennial dedication of the Church to the wisdom of revealed truth, the goodness of moral excellence, and the holiness of Divine worship. The following essays indicate, if nothing else, how far the author has yet to travel into the life of that Wisdom in whose eternal presence all times and places are.

Introduction

THE SEVENTIETH birthday of Father Matthew L. Lamb provides an occasion for honoring his work by the publication of these essays reflective of the central themes of his lifetime of prayer and intellectual labor. After studying under Bernard Lonergan, Karl Rahner, and Johann Baptist Metz, Lamb held professorships at Marquette University and Boston College for over thirty years. He is presently Professor of Theology and the founding Director of the Graduate School of Theology at Ave Maria University.

In this years immediately following Vatican II, as Lamb has shown, the framework of "liberal" and "conservative," adopted by theological popularizers to make intelligible to the mass media the complex theological discussions ongoing during and after the Council, became dominant within academic Catholic theology. These distortive categories stimulated a further ideologically driven popularization of Catholic theology by playing into the weaknesses of theological education after the Council. As Lamb has documented in various writings, students during this period generally entered Catholic theological graduate programs without knowledge of Latin or Greek and with little background in the philosophical and theological achievements and debates of the centuries prior to the twentieth. To compound the problem, increasingly the professoriate at the doctorate-granting Catholic universities in the United States had earned their doctorates at Protestant or secular programs (Chicago, Yale, and so forth), where training in the Catholic tradition was minimal. The results of these various trends are still very much with us, most notably the superficial engagement with the theological and metaphysical achievements of the Fathers and scholastics that undergird the teachings of the great Councils.

Within this context Lamb's writings stand out as exemplars of the combination of *ressourcement* and *aggiornamento* that the Council had in mind. In summarizing his vision, we might begin with his participatory understanding of reality. Human life is not a succession of monadic moments, because God creates time (experienced as human self-presence) as a participation in divine eternity. Divine eternity is not endless, impersonal duration and extension, but rather is the Father, Son, and Holy Spirit, the perfect presencing of Wisdom and Love. God's Providence, which is the expression of his Wisdom and Love, unites all time in Christological and eschatological fulfillment. Thus the linear progression of temporal moments is not a series of negations marked above all by death. Lamb observes that the ancients could not account for suffering and death; it is in Christ Jesus that all suffering and death are redeemed. The Resurrection thus plays a central role in Lamb's thought, but not one that displaces the suffering of the Cross. By the Holy Spirit Christ Jesus calls all human beings to the fullest graced participation of human understanding and loving in divine Wisdom and Love, in which the higher participation takes up and fulfills, rather than negates, the lower.

Graced participation in the divine Wisdom and Love is the mode by which the Church, sacramentally constituted so as to mediate visibly and historically the immediacy of the presence of the Triune God, receives and interprets divine revelation. As sapiential participation in the realities revealed by divine Wisdom, the Church's dogmatic judgments of truth under the guidance of the Holy Spirit are sapiential, as opposed to dogmatism that stops at the level of concepts. Theological and exegetical judgments of truth require metaphysical and theological intelligence adequate to the realities of creation and redemption. To attain such achievements of graced intelligence we must attend to the insights of the patristic and scholastic doctors of the Church, whose metaphysical apprehension of immaterial realities and humble submission to Christ in the communion of the Church display the conversion necessary for sapiential understanding. Graced intelligence enables us to live according to what is highest in us—wisdom and charity rather than arbitrary power, violence, and domination—and thereby to unleash the transformative power of Christological and pneumatological orthopraxis in the world. As opposed to modern ideologies of power, this graced participation in the divine Wisdom and Love within the unity and solidarity of the Church grounds a truly liberative praxis and recalls us to what it means to be Catholic in a post-Enlightenment culture such as America.

While this brief summary is insufficient to display Lamb's achievements, we hope that it at least evokes the potential of Lamb's thought to assist Catholic theology in moving beyond what is, in academic circles at least, its present narrow vision. The book's seven chapters—published separately in the 1990s and presented here in their original form—have been chosen to illumine the key aspects of Lamb's thought, displaying along the way the range and depth of his appropriation of ancient and modern thinkers.

Chapter 1, "The Resurrection and Christian Identity as *Conversatio Dei*," begins by contrasting modern and premodern autobiographical understandings of personal identity. For Augustine and Teresa of Avila, personal identity is defined by relationships with God and other human beings; for Rousseau God is solely a "judging spectator," and personal identity is defined by dates and places. Similarly the confession of sins is found in all three autobiographies, but in Augustine and Teresa it signals God's compassion and redemptive work, whereas in Rousseau it belongs to the task of demonstrating that Rousseau himself is, on the whole, better than others. Rousseau's self-understanding has lost the aspect of the human person in conversation with a wise and loving God, and has thereby been profoundly narrowed. The result is a modern anthropology that seeks internally to dominate libidinal desires and externally to dominate other human monads through societal power. After noting Hegel's and Heidegger's efforts to overcome this situation, Lamb argues that the solution lies in recovering Augustine's understanding of time-as-presence in Book XI of *Confessions*. He differentiates this Augustinian understanding of time from Plotinian views, on the basis of Augustine's awareness of God's historical self-revelation. In particular, the Resurrection of Christ shows that the Triune God has created and redeemed time; there are no isolated monads, but rather all are united in God's Wisdom and Love, and each person is related in communion to every other person.

Chapter 2, "Nature, History, and Redemption," emphasizes that "nature" and "history" are not closed off to God's Wisdom, as happens in Newton's conception of God's extrinsic command over the time-space continuum. True "historical consciousness," Lamb proposes, involves neither idealist universalism nor empiricist historicism. Rather, true historical consciousness is "sapiential" in identifying all things as coming forth from the Wisdom and Love of God. Drawing connections between Newton, Descartes, Leibniz, and Hegel, he finds that these modern thinkers conceive of the movement of time as a process of negation rather than fulfillment, a "progress" that is the domination of the past. By contrast, Einstein's four-dimensional universe once again integrates space and time and opens up the possibility of retrieving the patristic and scholastic understanding of divine eternity as embracing the concrete totality of the spatiotemporal universe. Lamb links modern understandings of time with Spinoza's reductive theory of biblical interpretation, which excludes anything but analysis of texts and the effects on these texts on the will—thereby leaving out the communicative praxis of intelligent teaching, which in the case of Scripture includes the realities of God, faith, and prayer. Lacking these realities that comprise a genuinely "critical history" of Scripture, one is left with a history of oppressors and victims who have no recourse to justice and liberation. Lamb calls for a sapiential communicative praxis that builds upon faith, hope, and love so as to be able to hear and respond to victims of oppression from within the graced solidarity made possible by the Triune God's creative and redemptive presence.

Chapter 3, "Eternity and Time," honors Lamb's longtime colleague and friend, Ernest L. Fortin, AA. Observing that Augustine makes the key breakthrough to finite intelligence as an analogue to the infinite intelligence of God, Lamb compares this view to the conception of divine eternity in Plato, Aristotle, Parmenides, Zeno, and Plotinus. All of them, he shows, either radically separate or conflate the eternal divine being and the realm of temporality. The polarity is bridged by Augustine's recognition of both the immateriality of human intelligence and the ability of rational judgment to apprehend the concreteness of being. Inspired by the incarnation of the Word, in which the eternal manifests itself supremely in the temporal, Augustine demonstrates that immaterial intelligence may be distinguished from temporality without being radically separated from it; indeed, faith and charity enable human rationality to participate in the Triune God's infinite communion of Wisdom and Love. This participation of human rational self-presence in eternal divine presence is not an idealism but rather very much a historical and communal participation in the Triune God's creative and redemptive work. Whereas Boethius and Aquinas enrich metaphysically Augustine's perspective, Duns Scotus's conceptualism cuts off the participatory relationship between intellectual judgment and concrete beings and thereby forces Scotus to conceive of the eternity-time relationship in terms of the divine will. The extrinsicism that results leads to modernity's closed-off conception of "nature," the pietistic privatization of religious experience, mechanistic theodicy, and the supposition that truth is power. With Lonergan, Lamb concludes that the analogy from human intelligence to divine eternal intelligence serves to defend both the freedom and the meaningfulness of human history as a created participation in the divine Wisdom—a history whose ultimate end is not despair and death but sharing in Christ in the glory of divine communion.

Chapter 4, "The Eschatology of St. Thomas Aquinas," observes that modern eschatology often takes up its theme in terms of divine power and will. Just as modern science understands knowledge as power (over the ordering of nature), so also modern eschatology, particularly in its fundamentalist forms, aims at knowing the secrets of the endtime so as to master it. By contrast, Aquinas envisions eschatology in terms of divine Wisdom. Wisdom, Lamb notes, apprehends the ordering of all things to their proper ends. Aquinas's theology begins with the Triune God and then moves through creation and redemption to the Christological and pneumatological fulfillment of human beings in the Kingdom of God. His theology is thus a "wisdom," and his eschatology a "wisdom eschatology" whose goal is not to gain rationalistic control over the events of the endtime, but rather to understand the Christological and pneumatological patterns of fulfillment by which the Triune God brings his creatures to eternal life in him. The key to eschatology is not cosmic cataclysms of power, but rather the fulfillment of the patterns of divine Wisdom by the transformation of the whole creation.

In this way Aquinas's analogous knowing of the Triune God as the Father's generation of the Word and the Father and Son's spiration of the Holy Spirit as Love, an analogous knowing that relies upon the light of faith and apprehending the absolute simplicity and unity of divine Wisdom and Love, undergirds his eschatology. Without the light of faith, the ancient philosophers had tended to see the sensible realm as evil in contrast to the intelligible realm. The light of faith exposes how divine Wisdom, in permitting the evil of spiritual pride on the part of rational creatures, can bring good out of evil not through power but through love in the Paschal Mystery of Christ Jesus. In his human knowledge on the Cross Christ knew and loved each and every one of us, and so he was able to bear not sins and sufferings in the abstract, but *our* sins and sufferings.

Already in Christ's Resurrection God has redeemed our histories of sin and suffering. Against Cartesian dualisms that envision the body as a mere machine moved by the soul as well as materialism that envision the human person as a mere machine, wisdom eschatology affirms the importance of the resurrection of the body, the redemption of the fullness of human personhood. The resurrection is an event that takes place for every individual, and does so within the communal context of the raising of the entire Mystical Body of Christ.

Wisdom eschatology is thus not derailed by the materiality of creation, by privileging the species over the individual or vice versa, or by sin and suffering. Faith, hope, and charity guide us to affirm that death does not have the last word, but rather divine Wisdom, in the risen Lord, establishes all things in justice. This justice is no mere act of arbitrary divine power, but rather is the divine Wisdom allowing for the freedom of rational creatures, even where that freedom has sought violently to frustrate its own orientation toward the Good, thereby causing its own punishment. The blessed find a glorious fulfillment, not merely a repetition of earthly life: Their highest powers of knowing and loving receive the immediate interpersonal presence of the Triune God that is the "beatific vision," and their lower powers participate in this unimaginable intimacy and joy through an "iconic" imaging of God in Christ. In this ever greater participation in the divine Wisdom, the blessed—not an abstract "countless" mass but each individually and personally known and loved by the Triune God—will know the meaning of the history of sin and suffering, and will rejoice in their communion with the Triune God and with each other.

Chapter 5, "Modernism and Americanism Revisited Dialectically: A Challenge for Evangelization," responds to Pope John Paul II's call for a new evangelization. Lamb begins by identifying three kinds of differences: complementary (e.g., husband and wife), genetic (e.g., seed and plant), and dialectical (e.g., truth and falsehood). According to some interpretations, he notes, Vatican II has blessed as complementary or genetic the differences between "modernism/Americanism" and Catholicism that were previously condemned by the Church as dialectical. Undifferentiated opposition has now become, on this view, undifferentiated affirmation. In response, Lamb first summarizes the differences identified by Leo XIII in *Testem Benevolentiae* (1899) and by Pius X in *Pascendi* (1907). These differences—among them agnosticism and immanentism regarding human ability to know God, the privatization of faith, dogmas as symbols or myths, dispensing with external and historically visible mediations in favor of individual guidance by the Holy Spirit—are clearly "dialectical." Lamb then proposes that Vatican II models a process of dialectical differentiation that sifts modernity's wheat from its chaff. A key element of this dialectical differentiation, he finds, consists in the Council's *communio* ecclesiology, "the mediation in truth of interpersonal immediacy," which is then further developed by John Paul II's encyclicals. This ecclesiology is not a "restorationist" project, as the "conversative versus liberal" reading of the Council would have it. Rather the Council and John Paul have committed themselves to restoring or uniting all things in Christ Jesus by means of deepening human beings' union with the Trinity through the missions of the Word and the Holy Spirit, the immediate interpersonal presence of the Triune God as mediated historically. This task requires taking seriously the beneficent influence of the light of faith upon human culture and the real existence of "dialectical" differences between Catholicism and Enlightenment liberalism (in its American incarnation), rather than assuming that all differences have become complementary or genetic. The Church offers hope to a world that otherwise assumes that dominative power trumps wisdom and individual freedom trumps the common good.

Chapter 6, "Inculturation and Western Culture: The Dialogical Experience Between Gospel and Culture," points out that "culture" is often separated from "nature" and that both are conceived as human constructs against human freedom. By contrast, a wisdom perspective affirms transcultural patterns that belong to spiritual and material nature and provide for measuring development as opposed to decline. Distinguishing his position from "extrinsic absolutism" on the one hand and "syncretism and parallelism" on the other, Lamb focuses on the historically and concretely (sacramentally) mediated immediacy and presence of the Triune God. Such mediated immediacy is difficult to understand in modernity due to the loss of a sapiential framework for institutional authority, which now appears as fragmented, arbitrary power. Lamb finds that in modern Western culture, therefore, the task of inculturation consists primarily in maintaining the mediating institution of the Church as more than a privatized voluntary association. In order to do this, however, theology needs both to overcome the polarization between reason and faith that threatens the mediated immediacy of the Triune God and to reclaim an understanding of "sublation" whereby development does not (as in Hegel) involve negation of what is prior. Lamb concludes by posing six issues for inculturation in the United States: (1) the United States as a fully post-Enlightenment culture; (2) the error of envisioning institutions as aggregates of monadic individuals and freedom as value-neutral; (3) the need for strengthening the Catholic identity of Catholic schools and hospitals; (4) the need for formation in the virtues; (5) the distinction between authoritarianism and authority; and (6) the centrality of holiness.

Chapter 7, "Communicative Praxis and Theology: Beyond Modern Nihilism and Dogmatism," observes that even if postmodernity is ultra-modernity, the difference is that the postmoderns are weighted by modernity's history of victims and no longer possess the supreme self-confidence that marked the Enlightenment period. By critiquing the thought of Max Weber, Lamb exposes the nihilistic "will to power" at the center of many modern conceptions of rationality and society. He then turns to Jürgen Habermas's "performative dialectics" and to Bernard Lonergan's *Insight: A Study of Human Understanding*. Building particularly upon Lonergan, Lamb develops three points with respect to a theologically informed communicative praxis. First, creative communication is not an act of violence and domination, but is creative precisely as an expression of wisdom and love. Second, creative communication with the past, solidarity in the Body of Christ, requires appreciating how the orthodoxy of the early Councils was shaped not by power but by Athanasius's resistance to imperial power out of faith and love for Christ Jesus. Third, after the Enlightenment's tendency to equate religious truth with domination, it must be asked whether modern secularism has in fact projected onto faith its own abuse of reason. Without discerning the normative achievements of the past, reason will be used to destroy reason, as in the Holocaust. Indeed, human rationality alone is not sufficient. As Lamb says, "No mere theory can console the suffering, no concept can raise the dead." Rather than continuing to bracket religious truth claims, modernity must recognize that only the theological affirmation of God's infinite wisdom and love can suffice to ground communicative praxis that truly opposes ideologies of power.

This introduction has only limned the surface of Lamb's integration of the theology of Trinitarian theology, theological anthropology, Christology, ethics, and eschatology, as well as his ability to unite biblical, patristic, scholastic, modern, and contemporary discussions.

1

The Resurrection and Christian Identity as *Conversatio Dei*

HE CHRISTIAN FAITH in the resurrection of Jesus Christ from the dead asserts the fundamental victory of Christ over the powers of death. To understand how faith in the resurrection influenced Christian identity, it is important to realize how contracted the modern experience of identity has become.

Johann Baptist Metz has exposed the tyranny of the time continuum over modern consciousness and life.[1] Modern identity seems to be pinned to an ongoing continuum of time from the past through the present into the future. This evolutionary worldview is simply taken for granted as the only identity capable of living up to the demands of historical consciousness. In fact, however, it is a myth that alienates modern identity from history for history is far more than some inexorable movement from past to future. History and human identity has been alienated into metaphors of mechanical movement under the supposed tyranny of space and time.

A striking difference between modern and premodern notions of identity can be seen in how we moderns identify so strongly with places and times. As an illustration, compare St. Augustine's and Rousseau's *Confessions* and St. Teresa of Avila's *Life*. Augustine praises God, so that his work is an

---

This essay was originally published as "Resurrection and Christian Identity as *Conversatio Dei*" in *Concilium: An International Journal of Theology* (October 1993): 340–55.

[1] Johann B. Metz, *Glaube in Geschichte und Gesellschaft,* 5th ed. (Mainz: Grünewald, 1992), 149ff.; idem, "Ohne Finale ins Nichts," *Frankfurter Allgemeine Zeitung,* 13 July 1991.

expression, as all created beings are, of God's goodness. Evil is evidence, not of any failure on God's part, but of human pride and sin. Specific dates and places do not figure significantly in Augustine's *Confessions*. Rather, his entire life, with all of its stages, is woven into an intensely interpersonal dialogue or conversation with God. From the fourth through the sixteenth centuries this orientation in autobiography was consistent. Teresa of Avila's *Life* has many passages of direct dialogue with God. While there are more references to interpersonal relations with family and friends than in Augustine's *Confessions*, there is a similar attention to those realities and relations without dwelling on specific times and places.

In the eighteenth century Jean-Jacques Rousseau's posthumously published *Confessions* set the typically modern genre of autobiography, beginning each section with the relevant years, starting with his birth in Geneva in 1712. Every few pages there are specific places and dates provided. At the opening the appeal to God is not a preview of a recurrent dialogue between Rousseau and God, for that does not occur in the twelve long books. Rather it is more like an oath invoking "my Sovereign Judge" and attesting that "I have bared my secret soul as Thou thyself hast seen it, Eternal Being!" God is not a conversation partner in Rousseau's life, but rather a judging spectator.

All three of these texts begin with confessions of personal sins and wickedness, but in Augustine and Teresa the context is one that understands sin and evil as contractions of their conscious living, as sad and ignorant meandering from the Divine Presence with whom they are now conversing. Confession is primarily praise and joy, and the honest admission of their sins is only to manifest how gracious and compassionate God is in continuing to love and redeem them. Their self-esteem is graced, opened as it is now into the very life and love of Father, Son, and Spirit. Human identity is experienced as conversational, and the most profound conversation is that between Augustine, Teresa, and God. History is not movement but conscious conversation and communion. History is most profoundly prayer.

For Rousseau the confession of his wretchedness and sins is quite different, almost contrary. He is going to trump his detractors by revealing his sins in a dare with all others: "But let each one of them reveal his heart at the foot of Thy throne with equal sincerity, and may any man who dares, say 'I was a better man than he.'" In effect, Rousseau initiates the modern, secular confessional genre. If a god is invoked at all, it is very much in *loco judicis.* There is no hint of a real friendship with God, only that "He" is on a judging throne. Interpersonal relations are confined to space and time as containers and markers. Nature with its geography and chronology become the context in which Rousseau performs his egophany:

> My purpose is to display to my kind a portrait in every way true to nature, and the man I shall portray will be myself. Simply myself. . . . I am made unlike any one I have ever met; I will even venture to say that I am like no one in the whole world. I may be no better, but at least I am different. Whether Nature did well or ill in breaking the mould in which she formed me, is a question which can only be resolved after the reading of my book.[2]

Rousseau concludes his *Confessions* with the very egophanic assertion that if anyone disagrees that he is an honorable man, that person ought to be "stifled." For Rousseau there is the impersonal "nature" that commands all. God is but another cipher of this cold nature. This is also an excuse mechanism. Rousseau is no longer responsible. Nature made him the way he is.

These contrasts illustrate a rather massive shift in human self-understanding, a contraction of self-presence and interpersonal conversation to those persons available to our sensations and perceptions. The dead are remembered, but they are not addressed as present in the Mystery of eternal life, as they are in Augustine and Teresa.

Reality seems increasingly restricted to what can be dated and placed. Humans are hardly made in the image and likeness of anyone else, let alone God. Rather, we humans are all locked into our own individuality within an impersonal "nature" that removes responsibility. Identity becomes merely an epiphenomenon. It is within this context that reincarnation appeals to moderns. The time continuum will save us eventually as we pass through many lives.

Indeed, the contracted modern identity has constructed a god in its own image. Just prior to Rousseau, Newton, Spinoza, and Leibniz had outlined the parameters of just such a god. Newton made space into a divine *sensorium* that permits all things to be present to God and allows God to be present in all things. Spinoza immanentized God to the point

---

2 Jean-Jacques Rousseau, *Confessions,* trans. J. M. Cohen (New York: Penguin, 1985), 17, 606.

that eternity is only ideational, as in "timeless truths." Thinking and extending seem to be the two main attributes of God.[3]

Leibniz pushed this by often identifying perception as conceptualization, thereby extending the derailed cognitional theories of Newton and Spinoza even further. We are, he forcefully argued, monads. "A genuine thing," for Leibniz, "must be individuated, monadized, through and through." Leibniz's theodicy articulates a God who enables each monad to revel in egophany insofar as God is *ens perfectissimum*:

> Every substance has something of the infinite, inasmuch as it involves its cause, God; it has even some trace of his omniscience and omnipotence; now in the perfect notion of any substance, if all of its predicates are included, the necessary and the contingent, past, present, and future; indeed any substance expresses the whole world according to its position [space] and its appearance [time].[4]

What Newton termed a divine sensorium, Spinoza a *natura naturans*, and Leibniz articulated in terms of his monadology and geometrical substance philosophy, Rousseau expresses autobiographically in a language to become usual for modern narratives of the self as conscious subject. The continuum of past, present, and future, of space and time, is the context in which monads participate somehow in a divine infinity, a *sensorium divinum*, *Deus sive natura,* or what have you. In, through, and with the continuum of space-time all monads have their substance and participate in infinity.

Wrongly extrapolating from mechanics, Leibniz tended to equate relations with forces. If relationships are forces, then the relations that really count are extrinsic rather than intrinsic. For whatever inner forces we have, the ones to "worry about" are those that might be stronger than ours. By the nineteenth century references to a God were perceived as less and less relevant to modern biography, psychology, sociology, and history—except as rhetorical flourish or as a symbol of premodern superstition.

This equation of relations with forces leads in two directions in our individualized, monadized modern world. One strand moves inward, the other outward. The inward strand delves into "psyche" and finds there the

3 Cf. A. Funkenstein, *Theology and the Scientific Imagination* (Princeton, NJ: Princeton University Press, 1986), 80ff.; Y. Yovel, *Spinoza and Other Heretics* (Princeton, NJ: Princeton University Press, 1989), 155, 213.

4 Cf. C. I. Gerhardt, ed., *Die Philosophische Schriften von Gottfried Wilhelm Leibniz,* 7 volumes (Berlin: Weidman, 1875–1890) vol. 7, 311 [my translation].

libidinal forces that "threaten" and make a mockery of our "thinking selves." The superego and the endopsychic censor must tyrannically keep these libidinal and death instincts in check as best they can (S. Freud). Desires are "ordered" only through forceful control, their natural state is disorder and chaos.

The other strand moves outward, to connect with modern theories of cunning force in society and politics from Machiavelli through Hobbes, Hume, and Locke to Marx and Weber. Social theory is control theory, and social power is domination *(Herrschaft)* in which those in authority give commands that are obeyed. Force is only overcome by force, so that freedom and peace, as well as order, can be guaranteed only through police and military forces. The natural state tends toward anarchy, disintegration. Laws seek to impose "order."

These are some of the dire consequences of the modern autobiographical identity shift. We tell our stories neither to share in a communion with our brothers and sisters nor to praise the reality of a gracious and compassionate God, but to engage in the competitive self-grounding or self-assertion characteristic of modern secularist contractions of consciousness to space and time (= objective) known with sensation and perception (= subjective).[5]

What I have been discussing until now is the aberration or cover story, which, in my judgment, has tended to derail modern experiences and expressions of autobiography, of the conscious time-span in which we narrate our memories and give voice to our expectations. Modern identity to that extent is contracted, truncated to space and time. From a horizon in which a St. Augustine or a St. Teresa could engage in the narrative of their lives as ongoing conversations with a Divine Friend, we move to the flow of Rousseau's narrative in which God functions intermittently as a harsh judge, but in which the continuum of space and time become all important as the horizon defining reality and fact. We have seen how immediate predecessors of Rousseau had conferred a divine status on extension and duration. Soon that status could be dispensed with, just as it had in empirical science. The absence of God in modern cultures is complete. One could explore Proust's *À la recherche du temps perdu* as the twentieth-century apotheosis of modern autobiography become novel, as such also the longing it expresses for an eternity transcending—embracing all time. Presence seeks a time where all dates are left to the remembrance of Another.

---

5 Cf. Richard Rorty, "Habermas and Lyotard on Postmodernity," in R. Bernstein, ed., *Habermas and Modernity* (Cambridge, MA: MIT Press, 1985), 161–75.

For many the reality of events does not depend upon their being recorded exactly in place and time. Measurement and movement are not criteria for the really real. Much more reality is accorded to intersubjective presence and interpersonal conversation. Notice how mothers tend spontaneously to narrate events relative to the births of their children.

Only if instrumental rationality triumphs does the clock tend to dissociate time from human events, from interpersonal encounters. So it is not surprising that Rousseau would seek to render his narratives "realistic" by dating and placing his memories. Modern individuality, with its monadic pretensions, underlies modern autobiography and first-person narrative novels.

Even the philosophical efforts to do justice to time and history ontologically, from Hegel through Heidegger, tend to juxtapose individuality and universality, *Eigentlichkeit* and *Allgemeinheit*, as though one necessarily negates aspects of the other. Objective time of universal process can be "subjectified" only by making the subject, with Hegel, absolutely objective *Geist*, or, with Heidegger, by denouncing this project as a denial of the subject's ultimate being-toward-death and finitude. In neither of these types of options is there recognized a concrete intelligibility of space and time embracing all of the extensions and durations in their concrete particularity.

The emergence of human beings with their histories marks the emergence of constitutive meaning, of human beings whose self-presence and intersubjective presence and interpersonal conversations involve a qualitatively new and different time: the time of our "now," of our personal and communal self-presence with its memories and expectations. The human experience of time is not of discrete instants on a mechanically imagined continuum, but of a time-span that resists the easy generalizations of the empirical sciences, which is as concrete and unique as each of us in both our personal histories and in our intersubjective and interpersonal conversations. Time becomes history.

What is the *reality* of history? If historical consciousness and critical history are discoveries of modern culture, we moderns are far from having understood adequately just what it is we have discovered. Insofar as historians date events, the use of time as movement is relatively unproblematic. History raises more questions as we explore just what is real history and what is not. The point of Augustine's eleventh book of his *Confessions* is not that measurement runs up against a neo-Kantian *aporia* or dilemma, but that measurement is simply unable to ground the reality of time-as-presence:

It is now, however, perfectly clear that neither the future nor the past are in existence, and that it is incorrect to say that there are three times—past, present, and future. Though one might perhaps say: "There are three times—a present of things past, a present of things present, and a present of things future." For these three do exist in the mind, and I do not see them anywhere else: the present time of things past is memory; the present time of things present is attentive reflection; the present time of things future is expectation. If we are allowed to use words in this way, then I see that there are three times and I admit that there are. Let us go further and say: "There are three times—past, present, and future." It is an incorrect use of language, but it is customary. Let us follow the custom. See, I do not mind, I do not object, I find no fault, provided that we understand what is said—namely, that neither what is to come nor what is past is now in existence. It is not often that we use language correctly; usually we use it incorrectly, though we understand each other's meaning.[6]

The reality of history is glimpsed in human presence. The reality of history is known in an ongoing conversation, a dialogue down through the ages, in which the time-span embraces all of humankind. By "mind" Augustine does not mean a monadic, individual mind, but the individual as at one with the human species *(anima)* and all human minds. When we say that such and such a human event happened at such and such a time, we are making a historical judgment. The past event no longer exists in time. And our judgment that it either did or did not occur is based, not on our own perception of the event itself, but on a complex set of beliefs and judgments that make up historical experience. The reality of the past, as of the future, is experienced, understood, and known in the ongoing time-span of human presence.

This is not an idealism, for the present of the past is a series of sublating operations of historical experience through historical understanding to historical judgment. Of course, neither Augustine nor any other premodern knew of critical history. They did not know how to move from history as presence to the many self-correcting processes of learning that make up critical historical knowledge. In judgment the historian is not "re-enacting" the past (à la Collingwood), instead the historian is grasping that there is sufficient evidence to state that such and such did or did not occur.

---

[6] St. Augustine, *Confessions* XI, 20.

When historical judgments require close attention to empirical data of sense, as in the first phase of critical history, the status of historical judgments will be the same as that of the empirical sciences. When normative historical judgments require attention to the data of consciousness, then it is possible to attain more than "the best available opinion," for mind is not simply a concept or idea, it is a reality each person in conversation embodies.[7]

The presence of the past is *memoria*, the presence of the future is *expectatio*; both are *praesens* in the present of the "attentive reflection" constitutive of the human present. The notion of presence as memory, attention, and expectation is not simply that of only one person, but, as just mentioned, of all concrete patterns of personal and communal and human specieswide operations down the ages.

Time as presence sublates time as the measure of motion. The vast expanse of extension and duration in the material universe is not, however, denigrated in a purely spiritual ascent, as with the Platonists and Manicheans. Those who interpret St. Augustine as only Platonist misread his texts.[8] No Platonist, especially a Plotinus, would, at the very height of the intellectual and mystical experience of the transcendent God, break into a prayer at how it is precisely in this experience of "God as Truth where, Oh God you feed your people Israel with the food of truth."[9]

Indeed, Augustine makes clear how his intellectual conversion moves far beyond what any of the Platonists could sustain. For when he narrates in Book VII of his *Confessiones* what he has learned from the Platonists, he never quotes them but only Scripture.[10] We come into the presence of God in himself, as St. Augustine writes, when God speaks God's own Word to us, in a flash of graced understanding, we touch the Eternal Wisdom who creates and redeems all reality.

This intense spiritual immediacy of God is precisely the experience we shall have when we share in the Resurrection of Christ.[11] To know the reality of the Risen Christ is precisely the grace of faith that, far from dark-

---

[7] Cf. Bernard Lonergan, SJ, *Method in Theology* (New York: Herder & Herder, 1972), 175–234.

[8] The first and third volumes of Paul Ricoeur's *Time and Narrative* (Chicago: University of Chicago Press, 1984–88) offer a neo-Kantian interpretation of Augustine's understanding of time that distorts its ontological meaning.

[9] St. Augustine, *Confessions* IX 10, with reference to Psalm 79:2 [my translation].

[10] Cf. James J. O'Donnell's three-volume study *Augustine Confessions* (Oxford: Clarendon Press, 1992), especially vol. II, 413.

[11] St. Augustine, *Confessions* IX, 10.

ening or blinding our intelligence, enlightens and strengthens it. As Augustine saw so clearly, only the theological virtues of faith, hope, and agapic love could keep the intellectual and moral virtues from declining into cynicism and stoicism.

The Resurrection clearly indicates how the goodness of the material universe is present in the eternal creative and redemptive presence of God. St. Augustine's grasp of God's eternal presence—an understanding that is further articulated in Boethius and St. Thomas Aquinas—is neither a Platonist nor a Plotinian conception of a timeless negativity. For Augustine God's eternal presence embraces through creation and the missions of the Son and Spirit the concrete totality of all times. There is no past and future in God, but only an eternal presence in, by, and for whom all times are created.[12] The opposition and dualism between divine eternity and time that both classical and modern philosophers have erected make it difficult for contemporary philosophers and theologians to recover the achievements of Augustine.[13]

Contrary to a Spinoza or Ricoeur, the *Totum Esse Praesens* or Totality of Existence as Presence in St. Augustine's understanding of God's creative and redemptive presence does *not* negate time but creates all times.[14] Far from an abstract universality of Concept or Thought, the Eternal Presence of God embraces and redeems all of creation, including the totality of human history. This is not an eternity that negates suffering. Rather all the evil and violence brought about by sin is transformed into the only genuine kingdom of justice and love.

There are no nameless victims of history. Each and every human being is known and loved by God. And it is only such infinitely wise love that guarantees justice and mercy in the face of human evil. Far from negating human freedom, God's eternal creative presence enables human freedom. To imagine that because God eternally knows each and every event of our

---

[12] Cf. Matthew L. Lamb, "Presence and Eternity in St. Augustine" (forthcoming). The new readings of Augustine will indicate, for example, how the paradigm operative in Augustine is far more informed with the Jewish and Christian biblical paradigms than previously thought, cf. Johann B. Metz, "Theologie als Theodizee?" in Willi Oelmüller, ed., *Theodizee—Gott vor Gericht?* (Munich: Wilhelm Fink Verlag, 1991), 103–18.

[13] John M. Rist, *Augustine: Ancient Thought Baptized* (Cambridge University Press, 1994), 290–313; Robert Dodaro and George Lawless, eds., *Augustine & His Critics* (New York: Routledge, 2000)

[14] See St. Augustine, *Confessions* XI, 11.

lives, God thereby imposes some necessity upon us as we live and decide in history is, as Augustine, Boethius, and Aquinas saw so well, a terrible category mistake. It is to imagine eternity as somehow "before" or "after" any event in history.[15]

The theological failure to grasp the achievements of Augustine, Boethius, and Aquinas by subsequent theologians led to the nominalist abstraction of a decisionistic God, which then later was transmuted into the abstract universality of the Enlightenment "Nature" as discussed at the beginning of this essay.[16] Recent studies indicate how it is precisely the abstract universality of the Enlightenment—and not genuine Christianity—that overshadows the modern horrors such as anti-Semitism.[17] Only the interpersonal presence of all humans in God can constitute the concrete universality mediated in and through the particularity of each and every person, event, thing.

The concrete universality of all of history in the Triune God grounds human and interpersonal solidarity in which each and every individual human being is understood as intrinsically related to all other members of the human species. There is no abstract notion of "nature" as an impersonal force behind all events. This abstract "nature" of the Enlightenment *philosophes* is the context in which human beings from other nations or races are viewed as "others" against those of our nation or race. The abstract nature also, as Hegel formulated so well, set the stage for the relations between one's own and the others in terms of domination and conflict.[18]

By ignoring and denigrating the specifically *theological* import of God's revelation in the Jewish and Christian covenants, modern cultures have failed to grasp that the absolutely transcendent and totally "other" God knows and loves all of creation into being. As St. Augustine and the entire Christian orthodox traditions emphasize, the whole of creation is good. Evil is not from the wholly other God, but is the product of free,

---

[15] For a recovery of the systematic significance of Thomas Aquinas on Divine Presence and human freedom, cf. Bernard Lonergan, SJ, *Grace and Freedom: Operative Grace in the Thought of St. Thomas Aquinas* (New York: Herder & Herder, 1971).

[16] Cf. Edith Wyschogrod, *Spirit in Ashes: Hegel, Heidegger, and Man-Made Mass Death* (New Haven, CT: Yale University Press, 1985), 94ff.

[17] Cf. Zygmunt Bauman, *Modernity and the Holocaust* (Ithaca: Cornell University Press, 1989); Paul L. Rose, *Revolutionary Anti-Semitism in Germany: From Kant to Wagner* (Princeton, NJ: Princeton University Press, 1990); Frank E. Manuel, *The Broken Staff: Judaism Through Christian Eyes* (Cambridge, MA: Harvard University Press, 1992).

[18] Cf. Wyschogrod, *Spirit in Ashes,* 106ff.

intelligent creatures refusing to live as the intelligent, good, and holy people God intends. All sin is a violent refusal to respond in life and praxis to
the divinely willed beauty and order of creation. Bereft of this faith, modern philosophers and anthropologists have continued to ignore the distinction between human nature as good and the evil that humans commit.
So all the horrors of history, all the violence that is sin and evil, are
ascribed to nature. Humans are "naturally" evil, prone to violence and
crime. Only the threat and use of coercion and death can check these supposedly natural tendencies.

What Jewish and Christian revelation unfold as sin is now ascribed to
nature, which supposedly "enlightened" states with secular education and
law enforcement will counteract as best they can.[19] What St. Augustine
saw with regard to the Roman empire applies to all efforts to deal with
human history apart from the theological virtues of faith, hope, and
agapic love: All kingdoms seek to domesticate the *libido dominandi*—the
lust for domination—by the use of force and the threat of death. And so
the reign of sin and domination continue.[20]

This abstract presence of nature or history is precisely not the Divine
Presence revealed in the passion, death, and resurrection of Jesus Christ as
the Second Person of the Trinity incarnate. The resurrection cannot be
affirmed apart from our faith in Christ Jesus. Like all the mysteries of our
redemption, it seals our identity as ever more profoundly called to a loving
conversation with the Triune God who alone can bring good out of evil,
just as God alone can create. Only in the kingdom preached and incarnate
in Jesus Christ do we have a kingdom of genuine understanding and love.[21]

The resurrection of the Jesus who went about healing and forgiving is
the epiphany of his Divine personhood. The great doctrinal distinction
between nature and person indicates how all human persons are called
into a communion and solidarity that far transcends the narrow confines
of monadic individualism. For no one can answer the question, "Who am
I?," except by narrating all the other persons from whom they were born,
with whom they have lived and are living. No one can narrate who he or
she is without reference to others whose being and friendship is integral to

---

19 Cf. Anthony Giddens, *The Nation State and Violence* (Berkeley: University of California Press, 1989); René Girard, *Things Hidden Since the Foundation of the World,*
   trans. Stephen Bann and Michael Metteer (Stanford, CA: Stanford University
   Press, 1987).
20 St. Augustine, *De Civitate Dei,* Books XIV and XIX.
21 Ibid., Book XXII.

his or her own personhood. Every autobiography is ipso facto a hetero-biography. The I and the other are in communion whether acknowledged or not. We shall not fully understand and know who each one of us is until we understand and know each and every human person who ever has, is, or will be a member of the human race.

Understanding and knowing all human persons will then bring us to the mystery of the Word Incarnate, Christ. This truly human being is a Divine Person. The totality of human persons is not fully understandable and knowable in themselves. As human persons we are all radically from Another in whom we live and move and have our being. In the Mystery of the Resurrection humankind will experience the redeemed goodness of the whole of creation.

CHAPTER 2

Nature, History, and Redemption

BERNARD LONERGAN, in his essay "Revolution in Catholic Theology," discusses the major changes that historical consciousness requires of Catholic theology. The concern for interiority and self-appropriation make large demands that could be said to revolutionize Catholic theology. Surprisingly Lonergan ends his essay by stating that this revolution is also a restoration, for it will enable theologians to understand the great achievements of the past. Lonergan concludes the essay on the revolution in Catholic theology by writing:

> To theology as governed by method and as an ongoing process the present situation points. If that pointing is accurate and effective, then the contemporary revolution in theology also will have the character of a restoration.[1]

There is an aspect of this revolution in theology, which challenges modern Enlightenment and contemporary postmodern horizons to change. Indeed, taking historical consciousness seriously will enable us to restore a proper systematic appreciation of the relation of time to eternity. Some have been puzzled by the failure of many contemporary theologians and

---

This essay is the English original text that appeared in German as "Die Offenheit der Geschichte und die Dialektik von Gemeinshaft und Herrschaft" in Edmund Arens, ed., *Anerkennung der Anderen* (Freiburg: Herder, 1995), 167–92.

[1] Bernard Lonergan, SJ, *A Second Collection* (Philadelphia: Westminster, 1974), 231–38.

Christians to appreciate how Catholic doctrines challenge us to a deeper understanding of the human and historical condition. In this essay I wish to indicate how modern theories of nature and time have promoted misunderstandings that have led to a truncation of consciousness to the data of sense, with the result that moderns and postmoderns are unable to measure up to scientific advances in the understanding of nature and time.

As Helmut Peukert asserts, there is the openness of history, in anamnestic solidarity, to redemption. The past is not closed off, any more than is the future.[2] Redemption can be systematically understood only if nature and history are understood as both ordered wholes, so that one has an ontology or metaphysics open to the new.

We have yet to grasp the fullness of how the four-dimensional universe uncovered by Einstein and Heisenberg[3] has deconstructed the Newtonian separation of space and time that deeply influenced the secularist truncation of modern historical consciousness. An irony of historicism is that it is a remnant, not only of nominalism, but also of a Newtonian worldview that played well into the prejudices of the Enlightenment's rejection of the past.

A fundamental issue in any systematic understanding of the human condition requires us to overcome the modernist truncation of modern horizons trapped in the false alternatives of either a conceptualist universalism, so typical of Kantian ethics, or the historicism of postmodern rejections of that universalism. These are merely two sides of the same failure to grasp the concrete universal, which Lonergan retrieved from the philosophical and theological orientations of classical Greek, Roman, and Christian medieval cultures.

With the false choices of an idealist universalism or an empiricist historicism, the past and tradition are effectively silenced in their ability to challenge and question our present. The dead are for all intents and purposes excommunicated. The human unity of communication is broken.

---

2 Cf. Helmut Peukert, *Science, Action, and Fundamental Theology*, trans. James Bohman (Cambridge, MA: MIT Press, 1984), 176–82, 202–45. Also his "Enlightenment and Theology as Unfinished Projects," in Don Browning and Francis Fiorenza, eds., *Habermas, Modernity, and Public Theology* (New York: Crossroad, 1992), 43–65.

3 Cf. Patrick Heelan, *Quantum Mechanics and Objectivity* (The Hague: Nijhof, 1968); Stephen Hawking, *A Brief History of Time* (New York: Bantam, 1988); Stephen Toulmin and June Goodfield, *The Discovery of Time*, 3rd ed. (Chicago: University of Chicago Press, 1982).

The conversation and debates that constitute the history of human civilizations, philosophies, religions is interrupted by a rejection of the past as "unenlightened," as hopelessly a product of "the dark ages."

The earnest dialogue, which constitutes genuine dialectics, is broken by too easy dismissals of the political and intellectual achievements of the past. There are many ways to silence the dead. The most usual is the "Besserwisserei" of moderns over ancients. Contradictory epitaphs witness to the distortions: The end of classical metaphysics is proclaimed while in the next breath it is accused of a forgetfulness of being; progress is proclaimed only to turn into nihilism with a happy ending.

Indeed, serious philosophical and theological transformations of historical consciousness uncover systematic distortions of communication in the Enlightenment privatization and negation of religious faith and practice. The loss of theology as a serious collaborator in the enterprise of the natural and human sciences has systematically distorted the efforts of the natural and human sciences in their practical tasks of transforming societies. Empiricism and instrumentalism are not just abstractions; with their loss of the classical difference between technique and praxis they are manifest in post-Enlightenment cultures that exalt the machine over the human. In all areas of politics, culture, art, and religion there is a dominance given to procedure over substance, to products over friendship, to roles and skills over virtues.[4]

A major reason for the mechanization and fragmentation of modern and postmodern cultures lies in the loss of wisdom. Modern science has vastly extended human knowledge of the empirical and particular. But there is no cognitive and philosophical mediation of the whole. The traditional task of wisdom, to order all things in light of the whole of reality, has been declared void.

This is the usual "end of metaphysics" dirges in modernity. Indeed, a danger in the modern period is precisely the tendency to see all ordering of things as springing, not from a love of wisdom, but from a disordered desire for power. Adorno's negative dialectics calls attention to the danger of a power-centered totality that is a lie. But metaphysics need not be defined by its abuse, any more than science or religion should only be

---

[4] Cf. Charles Taylor, *The Sources of the Self: The Making of Modern Identity* (Cambridge, MA: Harvard University Press, 1989); Alasdair MacIntyre, *After Virtue,* 2nd ed. (Notre Dame, IN: University of Notre Dame Press, 1984); Neil Postman, *Technopoly: The Surrender of Culture to Technology* (New York: Vintage Books, 1993).

defined by the abuses they have suffered. Today especially there is need of a metaphysics that can rescue the love of wisdom from the conceptualism and denigration of the powerplays of sinful human history. As I argued elsewhere, attention to the victims of history requires a mediation of the totality of history that is both intellectually compassionate and open to the transformation of the revealed Word of God.[5] For, as Bernard Lonergan writes, divine wisdom ordained, and divine goodness willed, not to remove the many evils afflicting human history through an exercise of power, but according the just and mysterious law of the Cross of Christ to transform, as only God can, all those evils into the highest good of the eternal life of the kingdom of God.[6]

How can a wise recovery of metaphysics be genuinely open to the new, which faith in the redemptive transformation of history requires?[7] How can the mediation of totality do justice to the vast diversity of history? One requirement will be a metaphysical wisdom capable of accounting for an understanding of time, which is open to messianic interruption and transformation.[8] One aspect of such a recovery will be to discover how the modern understanding of time has been derailed by an imaginative separation of time from space. What this separation did was twofold.

First, it made any wise understanding of time as an ordered totality of concrete durations impossible by insisting upon only the momentary and incessant becoming of these fragments of time. In some ways the modern Enlightenment version seemed commonsense enough. We can imagine the three dimensions of Euclidean geometry (height, width, and length), and we can see simultaneously all three dimensions. But we cannot imagine or visualize four dimensions, the dimensions of space *and* time, as in $ds^2 = dx^2 + dy^2 + dz^2 - c^2 dt^2$. These are highly intelligible, but not imaginable. Commenting on Newton, Stephen Hawking writes: "Time was completely

---

5 Cf. Matthew T. Lamb, *Solidarity with Victims: Towards a Theology of Social Transformation* (New York: Crossroad, 1982), 116–43.

6 Bernard Lonergan, SJ, *De Verbo Incarnato* (Rome: Gregorian University Press, 1964), 552–93. This will be published, with an English translation, as Volume 8 of his Collected Works by the University of Toronto Press.

7 This is the problem posed to metaphysics by Johann Baptist Metz. Cf. Sebastian Moore, *The Fire and Rose Are One* (New York: Crossroad, 1980), 94–96, 151–58; also his *Jesus the Liberator of Desire* (New York: Crossroad, 1989), 109–16.

8 Cf. M. Lamb, "Kommunikative Praxis und Theologie," in Edmund Arens, ed., *Habermas und die Theologie* (Düsseldorf: Patmos Verlag, 1989), 241–70. English version published in Browning and Fiorenza, eds., *Habermas, Modernity, and Public Theology*, 92–118.

separate from and independent of space. This is what most people would take to be the commonsense view."9

Second, instead of an ordered totality of concrete durations the Enlightenment commonsense view projected an imaginary and inexorable continuum of time moving from the past to the present into the future. Such a misunderstanding of time fits in well with a naturalism and historicism that can only conceive of order not as an intelligible pattern but as an exercise of dominative power and force. This owes much to Newton.10

The influence of Sir Isaac Newton on the development of modern mathematics and physics can scarcely be exaggerated. Less attention has been paid to his contributions to the seventeenth-century convergence of an empirical/mechanistically conceived science and theology.11 Michael Buckley has shown how Newton's universal mechanics, with its emphasis on motion and force, issues in a doctrine of God as the "Universal Commander" of a universe that is totally under divine domination *(dominatio entis spiritualis)*.12 The divine *sensorium* permits all things to be present to God and allows God's dominion to rule or command all things. Space as the *sensorium* of God privileges a Euclidean three-dimensional extension over time and duration. Space is always, but only moments of time are everywhere. There can be no ordered totality of concrete durations, so Newton relies on the fiction of absolute space and time. As he writes in the General Scholium to the second edition of his *Principia,* God

> is not eternity and infinity, but eternal and infinite; he is not duration or space, but he endures and is present. He endures forever, and is everywhere present; and, by existing always and everywhere, he constitutes duration and space. Since every particle of space is *always,* and every indivisible moment of duration is *everywhere,* certainly the Maker and Lord of all things cannot be *never* and *nowhere.*13

---

9 Hawking, *A Brief History of Time,* 18.

10 Cf. Bernard Lonergan, SJ, *Insight: A Study of Human Understanding* (Toronto: University of Toronto Press, 1992), 163–95.

11 Cf. the studies of Michael Buckley, SJ, *Motion and Motion's God* (New Haven, CT: Yale University Press, 1971) and *At the Origins of Modern Atheism* (New Haven, CT: Yale University Press, 1987). Also Amos Funkenstein, *Theology and the Scientific Imagination from the Middle Ages to the Seventeenth Century* (Princeton, NJ: Princeton University Press, 1986).

12 Buckley, *Motion and Motion's God,* 193–204; Buckley, *At the Origins of Modern Atheism,* 129–44.

13 Isaac Newton, *Principia,* ed. Florian Cajori, trans. Andrew Motte (Berkeley: University of California Press, 1934), vol. II, 545.

While there is an "always" of all space, there is not a corresponding "everywhere" of all time. Instead, only indivisible moments of time are everywhere, by which Newton means that at any instant of time the entire spatial universe exists. Totality is a characteristic of space, but not of time. One instant will follow another, but the three dimensions of space (width, height, and length) are simultaneously all present. Thus, even in Newton's discredited notions of absolute space and time, it is clear that space has a situational totality while absolute time flows successively.[14] That the imaginal matrix of Newtonian universal mechanics is spatial is evident in how "to order" for Newton is "to place."[15] Force and power moves things in space, and this is then projected infinitely onto God. Three-dimensional space is open to God's power, but does not manifest his wisdom. Time is *a fortiori* not open but closed in an inexorable continuum of fragmentary moments.

Although there are major differences between Descartes's quest for a universal mathematics and Newton's universal mechanics, these differences do not mean that Descartes was any less inclined to give priority to spatial simultaneity and order. The *res cogitans* ceded power to the *res extensa* time is merely thought, and so of lesser ontological value than space. Later, Leibniz, who rejected Newton's notion of absolute space, made explicit the fact that the past is past, gone, and so clearly separated a spatial order of nature, to which simultaneity applies, from the order of time, which is not:

> Given the existence of a multiplicity of concrete circumstances which are not mutually exclusive, we designate them as *contemporaneous* or *co-exiting*. Hence, we regard the events of past years as not co-existing with those of this year, because they are qualified by incompatible circumstances. *Time is the order of non-contemporaneous things.* It is thus the universal order of change in which we ignore the specific kind of changes that have occurred.[16]

What defines time is a non-simultaneity that is itself derived from a priority implicitly given to spatial simultaneity. Synchronicity is normative, and

---

[14] Cf. Lonergan, *Insight*, 181: "As absolute space, so absolute time is the result of looking for the absolute where the absolute does not exist."

[15] "Absolute, true, and mathematical time, of itself, and from its own nature, flows equably without relation to anything external, and by another name is called duration. . . . For times and spaces are as it were, the places as well of themselves as of all other things. All things are placed in time as to order of succession; and in space as to order of situation" (ibid., vol. I, 6, and 8).

[16] P. P. Wiener, ed., *Leibniz: Selections* (New York: Scribner, 1951), 201–2.

diachronicity is only derived, as constituted by mutually exclusive events. Instead of understanding time as an ordered totality of concrete durations, Leibniz projects a "universal order of change" in which the present and past are "mutually exclusive." The present cannot affirm or continue the past, but must exclude it. The Enlightenment prejudice against the supposedly unenlightened past is evident.

Hegel transposed the priority of space and time, but only by defining time as a totality that is abstract and ideal, the negative unity of being as becoming other than it is. Time is a momentary becoming, and so "Sie ist das Sein, das, indem es *ist, nicht* ist, und indem es *nicht* ist, *ist*."[17] The negativity constitutive of time is transposed into the centrality of negation in the process of historical sublation ("Aufhebung") in which the present can preserve and elevate the past only if it negates it as well. The genius of Hegel was to internalize all the contradictions of modernity into the ongoing dialectic of absolute spirit externalizing itself into history only to return to itself through the struggles and conflicts of history by the sublating power of absolute knowledge in which spirit knows itself.

The speculative Good Friday of the spirit foams forth, not in wisdom open to an ordered totality of concrete durations, but in a science that replaces contingency with the necessity of an inexorable logic of progress. Reality and truth are recognized only in "the certainty of the throne of Absolute Spirit."[18] Totality and order in Hegel are always dialectical, and dialectics is marked by the struggle for domination and recognition.

The contingent and particular is erased in the quest for a dominative totality. Individuality and universality are contrasted, *Eigentlichkeit* and *Allgemeinheit*, as though one necessarily negates aspects of the other. Objective time of universal process can be "subjectified" only by making the subject, with Hegel, absolutely objective *Geist*, or, with Heidegger, by denouncing this project as a denial of the subject's ultimate being-toward-death and finitude. In neither of these options is there recognized a concrete intelligibility of space and time as ordered totalities of concrete extensions and concrete durations in their particularities and novelties.[19]

Walter Benjamin's and Theodor Adorno's constellations, clusters of terms and images that render present some weak premonitions of redemption, open a path that requires more than the expressivist rejection of

---

[17] Hegel, *Enzyklopädie der philosophischen Wissenschaften*, §258.
[18] Cf. the end of Hegel's *Phenomenology of Spirit*.
[19] This is how Lonergan understands space and time, cf. *Insight*, 172–95.

totality and universality. Indeed, being faithful to the wisdom of those constellations, means rescuing them from the historicism and relativism that consigns those redemptive fragments to the "wreckage upon wreckage" which the angel of history longs to make whole.[20] Such "framing epiphanies," as Charles Taylor calls them, are too exposed to the nihilism that is so deeply ingrained in modern cultures.[21]

Space and time are ordered totality of concrete extensions and durations. This totality is the four-dimensional concrete universe in which both space and time, both nature and history, in all of their particular and unique things and events, exist. This means moving beyond the imaginal matrix that places the universe in a three-dimensional Euclidean framework with time as merely incidental. While we cannot imagine the four-dimensional universe of Einstein's special relativity, it is highly intelligible. Nor is it a totality that ignores or belittles the particular and unique, for the totality is known only as a heuristic anticipation of ordered things and events open to whatever occurs.[22] All time is included in this heuristic just as readily as all space.

This understanding of totality replaces continua of force and unilinear progress with freedom open to success and failure, both progress and decline. So, for example, the technological applications of special relativity in nuclear weapons has made abundantly clear that we humans will either renounce the international use of such force as a means of settling disputes or such force will destroy the possibility of human life on this planet. Nuclear weapons confront humankind with the need either to grow in wisdom and recognize the stupidity of violence or perish. What in fact will happen we do not know, we can only surmise various probabilities, and those are always open to revision. For example, who would have predicted the

---

20 Cf. Walter Benjamin, *Illuminations,* trans. Harry Zohn (New York: Schocken Books, 1978), 257–58: "This is how one pictures the angel of history. His face is turned toward the past. Where we perceive a chain of events, he sees one single catastrophe which keeps piling wreckage upon wreckage and hurls it in front of his feet. The angel would like to stay, awaken the dead, and make whole what has been smashed. But a storm is blowing from Paradise; it has got caught in his wings with such violence that the angel can no longer close them. This storm irresistibly propels him into the future to which his back is turned, while the pile of debris before him grows skyward. This storm is what we call progress."

21 Charles Taylor, *Sources of the Self* (Cambridge, MA: Harvard University Press, 1989), 468ff.

22 This is further analyzed in Bernard Lonergan's notion of emergent probability, cf. *Insight,* 126–62.

sudden collapse of the Soviet Union and the lessening of tensions regarding nuclear war? History is not locked into "iron laws" of nature or progress. Rather, both nature and history are open to both progress and decline.

A contemporary understanding of nature in the natural sciences since Einstein, and especially since Heisenberg's Quantum Theory, requires an openness to the statistical and change in a way that Newtonian mechanics could not allow.[23] As Kant simply transposed Newton's absolute time into an *a priori* form of human sensibility,[24] so Hegel broke with Kant's reliance on sensible intuition only to develop intellectual intuitions into a dialectic that is "conceptualist, closed, necessitarian, and immanental."[25] The closed Hegelian system left history in the inexorable continuum of time, now unfolding according to the necessary laws of the Absolute Spirit, among which was the struggle to the death of master and slave, and the negativity of war.[26] Little wonder, then, that some would see in the end of the Cold War a Hegelian intimation of the end of history.[27] The need to move beyond these modern, post-Enlightenment parameters is evident if political life is to overcome the violence that is fundamental to modern nation-states.[28]

In a four-dimensional universe where time is intrinsic to nature, and time is defined, not as only momentary, but as the ordered totality of concrete durations, then the openness of time and history becomes more evident. We can no longer separate the past from the present or both of them from the future. Indeed, from a theological perspective, we can appreciate how God's act of creation embraces the totality of the entire spatiotemporal universe. All of creation, including the totality of concrete durations with all

---

[23] Cf. Patrick Byrne, "Teleology, Modern Science and Verification" in Fred Lawrence, ed., *The Legacy of Lonergan* (Boston: Boston College Lonergan Institute, 1994), 1–45.

[24] Cf. Lonergan, *Insight*, 177–81.

[25] Ibid., 446.

[26] Cf. Edith Wyschogrod, *Spirit in Ashes: Hegel, Heidegger, and Man-Made Death* (New Haven, CT: Yale University Press, 1985), 148: "Using the struggle to the death as a paradigmatic pattern of Spirit's activity Hegel tries to show that war is necessary for the sublation of individual ego on behalf of the state, which he considers to represent a higher form of reason, and for states themselves, whose honor depends upon their willingness to risk their sovereignty. For Hegel war is not absolute evil but necessary for the life of polity."

[27] Francis Fukuyama, *The End of History and the Last Man* (New York: Free Press, 1992).

[28] Cf. Bruce Porter, *War and the Rise of the State: The Military Foundations of Modern Politics* (New York: Free Press, 1994).

of the events occurring in them, are present in the Divine Eternal Presence. Indeed, we now may be able better to understand the theoretical achievements of Augustine, Boethius, and Thomas Aquinas in their understanding of God's eternity as the total simultaneous presence of all that is. There is no "before" or "after" in God. In the Triune Presence the whole of the universe, and the whole of history, is present.[29] Similar to the four-dimensional universe, this understanding of eternity is highly intelligible, but not imaginable.

Failure to understand this systematic breakthrough led to the imaginable rhetoric, which opposed a "static eternity" to dynamic history. This breakthrough was neither Platonist nor Plotinian, for both of these imagine a contradiction between eternity and time. In Augustine, Boethius, and Aquinas, eternity does not negate but creates time: Eternity does not contradict but creates twice. Preaching eternal life Jesus was not denigrating time or history. As Augustine puts it, contrary to the Platonists, the eternal Word became man, revealing how the eternal God, as *totum esse praesens*, creates and redeems all time.

Nominalism paved the way for the Enlightenment to set eternal life in opposition to history, so that those seeking eternal life were despising the good life on earth. The Beyond as "Jenseits" was opposed to the here and now as "Diesseits." From this loss of a grasp of the simultaneous totality of time in God's presence, there was dissolution of time itself into a continuum of isolated moments. The present was set in opposition to the past. Memory and tradition were disparaged; the apocalyptic expectation that awaited the advent of the kingdom of God was emptied into what Metz calls a softened evolutionary eschatology.[30]

These all result from a faulty understanding of time and history, a failure to mediate a totality, which is genuinely open to the new without negating the old. The fixation of the Enlightenment upon the present moment, set up in opposition to the past, not only mirrored the hyperindividualism of autobiography in the Enlightenment (e.g., Rousseau's *Confessions*),[31] but also accounts for the emergence in Spinoza's *Theological Political Treatise* of the historical-critical methods.

---

[29] For further reflections on this, cf. chapter 1 above; also Frederick Crowe, SJ, "Rethinking Eternal Life," *Science et Esprit* 45(1 and 2; January–May 1993): 25–39 and 145–59.

[30] Cf. Johann B. Metz, *Glaube in Geschichte und Gesellschaft*, 5th ed. (Mainz: Grünewald, 1992), 149ff.; idem, "Ohne Finale ins Nichts," *Frankfurter Allgemeine Zeitung*, 13 July 1991.

[31] Cf. chapter 1 above.

Neither nature nor history is open for Spinoza. Both are fixed and necessary chains of events. Confronted with the religious pluralism of his day, Spinoza sought to privatize faith and show how the Scriptures were to be empirically studied, as nature is.

> I may sum up the matter by saying that the method of interpreting Scripture does not widely differ from the method of interpreting nature—in fact, it is almost the same.[32]

Such an interpretative study of the Scripture restricts itself to the texts alone. No appeal can be made to faith, for that is private and personal, sharply separated from reason.[33] Faith plays no role in the interpretation of Scripture, for the universal rule is to only accept as meanings of the texts what anyone can perceive from studying the history of that text. Spinoza makes clear that biblical interpretation does not concern itself with the truth of the texts, but only with perceptible meanings.

Thus the birth of the historical-critical methods is to treat the Bible as any other text. As Newton's mechanics sought only three-dimensional perceptible motions, so Spinoza's canons of interpretation recognize only those perceptible textual meanings found in the Scriptures as a perceptible book.

> We are to work not on the truth of passages, but solely on their meaning. We must take especial care, when we are in search of the meaning of a text, not to be led away by our reason in so far as it is founded on principles of natural knowledge (to say nothing of prejudices): in order not to confound the meaning of a passage with its truth, we must examine it solely by means of the signification of the words, or by a reason acknowledging no foundation but the Scriptures themselves.[34]

Spinoza here anticipates the deconstructionist insistence upon severe restriction to intertextuality—all we have is texts. Little wonder, then, that Spinoza would restrict faith to an obedience and piety, the assent of faith is only obedience, an act of will, and not an intellectual act. Theology is founded on

---

[32] Spinoza, *A Theological Political Treatise,* trans. R. Elwes (New York: Dover, 1951), 99.

[33] Ibid., 10: "Furthermore, as men's habits of mind differ, so that some more readily embrace one form of faith, some another, for what moves one to pray may move another only to scoff, I conclude . . . that everyone should be free to choose for himself the foundations of his creed, and that faith should be judged only by its fruits."

[34] Ibid., 101. Also Yirmiyahu Yovel, *Spinoza and Other Heretics,* volume II: The Adventures of Immanence (Princeton, NJ: Princeton University Press, 1989).

obedience to revelation and has no power to ever oppose reason. While philosophy and reason are only concerned with knowledge and truth, theology is totally separate, concerned only with obedience and piety. The teachings of the Scriptures, as Spinoza cynically remarks, need not be true, they need only promote pious and obedient acts.[35]

As Edmund Arens has shown, the dichotomy between teaching and action, between doctrinal content and text, between witnessing to the truth and confessing in word and deed, is impossible to maintain once one has taken seriously the constitutive meaning and truth of the communicative praxis of confessing the faith.[36] What is more, there is a failure to be genuinely and fully critical. The modern dichotomy between faith and reason fails to achieve the critical differentiations attained by Thomas Aquinas. What Spinoza evidences is how deeply nominalism has influenced modern dichotomies between intelligence and will, truth and commitment.

The openness of history is not an uncritical openness, a pious wish that has no intelligence. Quite the contrary. What Spinoza, and any exclusive reliance upon the historical-critical methods he pioneered, has done is to truncate the experience of history. To rule out of court the most important aspects of the genuine confession and practice of the Christian faith is not to promote a critical knowledge of history, but rather an ignorant one. The Enlightenment, instead of attending to the genuine witness of the martyrs and saints of the Church, turned rather to the abuses of religion. To define Christianity, or anything, by its abuses is not critical but prejudiced. Imagine if science or art were so judged.

The process of critical history open to the totality of events concretely occurring, as a process from historical experience to historical knowledge, not only deals with the meaning of texts, but also attends to which meanings are true, and what in fact are the realities to which the texts or events refer. As Lonergan points out, a fully critical historical process occurs twice. "In the first instance one is coming to understand one's sources. In the second instance one is using one's understood sources intelligently to come to understand the object to which they are relevant."[37] The first phase of critical his-

---

[35] Ibid., 182–99; cf. 185: "Lastly, it follows that faith does not demand that dogmas should be true as that they should be pious—that is, such as will stir up the heart to obey."

[36] Cf. Edmund Arens, *Bezeugen und Bekennen: Elementare Handlungen des Glaubens* (Düsseldorf: Patmos, 1989), 353–404.

[37] Bernard Lonergan, *Method in Theology* (Toronto: University of Toronto Press, 1992), 189; on objects, also 156–58, 161–62.

tory is the very familiar one of identifying authors or historical agents, situating their actions and/or works in time and place, studying their historical contexts and sources, and so on. But all of this is only in order to direct attention to what should be the critical historian's main objective—a second phase, aimed at "understanding the process referred to in one's sources."[38]

While a critical historian might not need to know faith, the spiritual life, or the Mystery of the Trinity to do textual criticism, establish sources, compare one set of texts with another set of texts (after all, anyone who can read can do that!), it is something else if he or she is going to engage in a history of faith, prayer, or theology as an *intellectus fidei*. If the critical historian has no knowledge of God, no familiarity with faith or prayer, with witness and confessing, then the critical historian is anything but "critical" in the full sense of that word.

The so-called critical historian is in fact an ignorant historian when it comes to the second phase of critical history. Then he or she is like a historian of mathematics who knows little about mathematics. Such a person might well be able to do a smash-up job comparing various mathematical texts, at dating and placing them more or less precisely, at working out certain social and/or cultural processes that were going on at the time the mathematical texts were being produced, at who used which text to get what advantage in this or that situation, how such a text was used in the production of weapons, what the weapons did, and the like. Undoubtedly, such a history would be very readable for those who are not interested in knowing the history of mathematics so much as in knowing what else was going on when such and such a mathematics was being done. But no one would claim that such a history would merit the name of a genuinely critical history of mathematics.

---

38 As an example, take autobiographies, a critical historian would set about situating Augustine's *Confessions*, Teresa's *Life*, Rousseau's *Confessions* in their very different historical, literary, cultural contexts, what sources they drew upon, what texts are more reliable, etc. This is fairly standard stuff in historical theology. One can read the results of such critical historical field work in the surveys and articles and books given to graduate students to introduce them to a subject, for example, Peter Brown's book on Augustine. But can the critical historian make the move to the second phase or instance of critical history when what an Augustine or a Teresa are so obviously discussing is their friendship with the Triune God? What is moving forward in the historical communities of the faithful who down the ages continue to read and meditate upon these works in their contexts of their own deepening friendship with God? Does Peter Brown do the kind of critical history that could make such a second step?

I am afraid not many genuinely critical histories of theology have been done yet. The sad thing is that what passes for critical histories are usually histories that are critical of theology, that simply assume that what is really real is a secular horizon in which it is at best a private opinion, and at worst a neurotic or psychotic delusion, that an Augustine or a Teresa were caught up in an ever-deepening friendship with Father, Son, and Spirit. Why is it that theology and religious studies are so lacking in self-knowledge that they alone, of all disciplines, now seem so ready to mistake ignorant histories for critical histories? This is hardly a *docta ignorantia*!

I am not stating that one must be moral or holy to write a critical history of morality or of the saints, any more than I am saying that one must be an alcoholic to write a critical history of alcoholism. I am saying that one must *know* the realities operative, the processes occurring, in morality, holiness, or alcoholism. Similarly, if one is going to prepare a critical history of faith, prayer, or theology, one had best know something about the realities of faith, prayer, or theology. Instead, what we have is a widespread conceptualism, and what I would call "comparative textology," à la Spinoza. A recognition of the openness of history requires a genuine theology in which faith and reason are neither separated nor confused, but in which they are properly differentiated.

Conclusion: The Redemption of Victims

History is open to the redemptive transformation of the kingdom of God revealed in the life, death, and resurrection of Jesus Christ. The openness of history posited by the theological works of all those who understand the fundamental importance of universal anamnestic solidarity with the victims of history is an openness that insists upon redemption that only God incarnate in Christ has offered humankind. One has to be fully realistic in the heuristic openness to the totality of all concrete things and events, persons and acts, throughout the whole of history.

This means a concrete heuristic that envisages all the goodness, joy, and justice, as well as all the horror, evil, and injustice that constitutes the ongoing history of the human race. It means recognizing that the innocent victims of injustice cannot receive full justice within the limitations of either life, as a biological span between birth and death, or the limitations of a good life, as the life of excellent cognitive and moral self-constitution by human beings. For neither life nor the good life can raise the dead, bring back the murdered millions whose blood has drenched each page of history. No communities of life or the good life can resurrect the dead victims of the empires of violence, dominative power, and death.[39]

Any fully realistic assessment of the evil in human history, how movements for justice and liberation turn into engines of injustice and oppression, can appreciate Max Horkheimer's comment: "Die großartigste Lehre in beiden Religionen, der jüdischen we der christlichen, ist . . . die Lehre von der Erbsünde. Sie hat die bisherige Geschichte bestimmt und bestimmt heute für den Denkenden die Welt. Möglich ist sie nur unter der Voraussetzung, daß Gott den Menschen mit einem freien Willen geschaffen hat."[40] The Enlightenment's rejection of theology has meant that the human sciences have studied men and women without the theological categories of sin and grace. Whatever evil humans do is then attributed to their human natures. So violence, war, and vice are taken as natural human attributes. Social policies and political regimes are built on such false premises, and so the violence, war, and evil are spread, compounded, and intensified by all the modern means of communication and force.

Given sin and the massive injustices in human history, the importance of holiness and the theological virtues cannot be overestimated in the tasks of a new wisdom-oriented enlightenment. The fact that theology has disappeared from the cultural patrimony of our post-Enlightenment intellectual establishment has meant that empirical science is bereft of the wisdom it so desperately needs. The empirical sciences are charting how human beings behave, how they act. They are ascribing that behavior—no matter how violent and sinful it is—to human nature. On the basis of such studies social policies are formulated, and so the violence and sin becomes structured into the society and culture.

In such cycles of social and cultural decline the intellectually virtuous tend toward cynicism, while the morally virtuous tend toward stoicism. The intelligent quest for wisdom and science, as well as the moral quest for justice, cannot succumb to cynicism and indifference. Because our kingdom is not of this world, we can dedicate ourselves to the creative and redemptive transformation of this world. Because through faith, hope, and

---

39 Cf. M. Lamb, "Christianity within the Political Dialectics of Community and Empire," in N. Biggar, J. Scott, and W. Schweiker, eds., *Cities of Gods: Faith, Politics and Pluralism in Judaism, Christianity and Islam* (New York: Greenwood Press, 1986), 73–100.

40 Max Horkheimer, *Die Sehnsucht nact dem ganz Anderen* (Hamburg: Furche Verlag, 1970), 64–65.

love we are in communion with the absolutely transcendent Triune God, we are members of one another in the historically immanent mediations of the missions of the Word and the Spirit to bring about the kingdom of God in our time and culture.

All understanding involves a suffering, a *pati*, and it is only when the light of our minds is healed and intensified by the light of faith that we can avoid the temptations to cynicism, skepticism, and despairing nihilism when, from all around us and deep within us, come the cries of the victims.

Only with the strength of the Spirit can the extended passion narratives of all of human history narrated in the new covenant be accepted as Gospel, as good news of salvation in the glory of the resurrection. Incorporated within the Paschal Victim are all the victims of history, some of whose stories grace us from the opening pages of Genesis to the last pages of Revelations. They teach us a wisdom that is of God, a wisdom of the Blessed "who have come out of great suffering and been washed in the in the blood of the Lamb. They shall neither hunger nor thirst nor suffer any more, for God shall wipe away every tear from their eyes" (Rev 7:14, 17). If the depth of human suffering is to birth understanding, it is because of the kenosis of the Divine Wisdom who alone can bring good out of evil, grace out of sin, life out of death. Only in the eternal kingdom of God will the empires of history be fully transformed into the justice and agapic love of the Triune God.

CHAPTER 3

Eternity and Time

A FUNDAMENTAL TENET of Ernest Fortin's learning and teaching—if not a basic orientation of his entire intellectual life—is the realization that classical philosophers and theologians can teach us lessons most important to contemporary culture and thought. Fortin's essays carry forward the ongoing debates between the ancients and the moderns, masterfully illustrating how many a modern genius failed to understand this or that classical thinker. There is no hint of archaism in Fortin's writings; he is not an archeologist of the past retrieving the ancients only to entomb their teachings in crusty museum reliquaries. Rather, Fortin is adept at showing the relevance of ancient wisdom to some of the most pressing issues of our time.

In this spirit, but without Fortin's finesse, this essay sketches contributions Christian philosophers and theologians made to an understanding of eternity and time. In his essay on "Faith and Reason in Contemporary Perspective," Fortin reflects on the relation of faith and reason, philosophy and theology, in the light of Robert Sokolowski's *The God of Faith and Reason*. He generally agrees with Sokolowski in the latter's criticisms of Karl Rahner and Bernard Lonergan for privileging the biblical "createdness of the world," and not giving "due recognition" to the pagan state of mind on this matter. Yet, for Fortin, Sokolowski does "not go all the way" in giving due

---

This essay was originally published as "Eternity and Time" in Michael P. Foley and Douglas Kries, eds. *Gladly to Learn, Gladly to Teach* (New York: Lexington Publishers, 2002), 195–214.

recognition to the pagan state of mind when he disagrees with Leo Strauss's ambiguity about religion and its relation to philosophy as a way of life. Indeed, in support Strauss's voluntaristic interpretation of biblical religion, Fortin invokes both the biblical lack of philosophical reasoning and the voluntarism of Scotus and Ockham. This was not a facile *post hoc propter hoc* argument; rather, Fortin wished to call attention to a little-known fact that Scotus and Ockham have influenced subsequent thought far more than Aquinas.[1]

This is hardly a major issue in Fortin's extensive work. It does illustrate well, however, his profound respect for the genius of Leo Strauss and his concern to make sure that the tension between faith and reason not be ignored. With non-believing intellectuals he would call attention to the enlightening influences of faith; with believing intellectuals he would sometimes question whether they had attended to the cogency of rational arguments without belief. Fortin appreciated Strauss's distinction between *entia* and *esse*, between "beings" and the "to be," the latter in the highest sense meaning "to be always." Prior to the seventeenth century, Strauss wrote, "philosophy had been the humanizing quest for the eternal order, and hence it had been a pure source of humane inspiration and aspiration."[2]

Among the students of Strauss few had the grasp of patristic and medieval thought that Fortin enjoyed. He sometimes criticized a tendency to lump all the medieval "scholastics" together, and to fail to take into account the vast differences, for example, between the theoretical positions of Thomas Aquinas and those of Scotus, Ockham, and the later schoolmen.[3] Facile notions of historical progress generally portray late medieval thought as a development of Aquinas's positions rather than an explicit counterposition or deviation. Yet, Scotus was no more a development of Thomas than Zeno was of Plato. As Strauss reminds us, return may be more demanding than progress.

---

[1] Cf. Ernest Fortin, *The God of Faith and Reason in Classical Christianity and the Political Order: Reflections on the Theologico-Political Problem,* ed. J. Brian Benestad (Lanham, MD: Rowman & Littlefield, 1996), 287–316, especially 301, 310–11.

[2] Leo Strauss, "Natural Right and the Historical Approach" in his *An Introduction to Political Philosophy: Ten Essays* (Detroit: Wayne State University Press, 1986), 122 and 124.

[3] A most recent illustration of this is Clark A. Merrill, "Leo Strauss's Indictment of Christian Philosophy," *The Review of Politics* 62 (2000): 77–105. For a better, more focused treatment of the questions involved, see James Schall, SJ, "A Latitude for Statesmanship? Strauss on St. Thomas," in Kenneth Deutsch and Walter Nicgorski, eds., *Leo Strauss: Political Philosopher and Jewish Thinker* (Lanham, MD: Rowman & Littlefield, 1994), 211–30.

A key element in discerning true retrievals and developments from sophistical derailments is the presence or absence of what in St. Augustine is "intellectual conversion"—that is to say, the realization of how the intelligible differs from the sensible. Though one can find this realization among the Greek and Latin Fathers, Augustine's reflections on the matter are relevant for an understanding of both time and eternity. Augustine had discovered aspects of a natural knowledge of God and of human reason that transformed what he had learned from his much-admired Platonic books, while his reflective grappling with the contingency of the universe led him to transcend pagan cosmogonies and cosmologies. Augustine thus serves as a good example of how Jewish and Christian theologians developed an understanding of nature and history, under the aegis of revelation, which would not otherwise have been accessible.[4]

I shall first sketch the context and intellectual exercise of understanding and judging as providing the analogue for a proper understanding of eternity and time. Then I shall outline theories of divine eternity in the achievements of Augustine, Boethius, and Aquinas. Subsequent thinkers like Scotus and Ockham, we shall see, did not measure up to the demands of intellectual conversion. Serious philosophy as metaphysics was invaded by a conceptualist logicism. That paved the way for nominalism and the conceptualism of modern times. Finally, I shall briefly touch on a return to the eternal and redemption of the quest for intellectual and moral excellence.

Intelligence in Act as Analogue

Augustine's intellectual conversion, as narrated especially in books five through nine of his *Confessions*, instilled an awareness of the importance, not only of understanding *(intellectus)* but also of judging that the understanding is true, of *Veritas*. The nature of mind for Augustine, as for Plato and Aristotle, is given and to be discovered: It is not self-constructed, as for many moderns.[5] Augustine narrates his conversion to Christ as integral to

---

[4] Fortin's regard and love for the genius of Augustine led him to remark time and again how faith and reason mutually enlighten each other when properly understood. For example, see Ernest Fortin, *The Birth of Philosophic Christianity: Studies in Early Christian and Medieval Thought*, ed. J. Brian Benestad, (Lanham, MD: Rowman & Littlefield, 1996), 169–250, and his "Augustine, Thomas Aquinas, and the Problem of Natural Law" and the three following essays in *Classical Christianity and the Political Order*, 199–286.

[5] Cf. Fortin, *The Birth of Philosophic Christianity,* 10–11.

his quest for intellectual and moral excellence. Truth is divine, and truth beckons intelligence to a love and understanding that both confirms and elevates human knowing and loving. So, at the beginning of Book VII of the *Confessions*, Augustine mentions how he was so "gross of mind" that he had not come to the realization of how the mind, while it generates all images, is not itself an image "but of a different nature altogether."[6]

Then, in chapter 17 of Book VII, Augustine reflects on the nature of human intelligence as it judges something to be true and another thing false. "So, as I reflected on how it was that I came to make these judgments which I did make, I discovered above my changing mind an unchanging and true eternity of truth." He then recounts how he ascended from sensible and corporeal things to the faculty of reason and the intelligible and intelligent light by which he is led to prefer the true and eternal to the changeable. That this was not a Cartesian thinking or idealist concept, Augustine then narrates that this intellectual conversion to truth is a discovery of Being: "And in the flash of a trembling glance my mind came to That Which Is. I understood the invisible through those things that were created." But he immediately adds that this discovery was not yet habitual. For he could not live the theoretic or contemplative life demanded by the discovery until Christ gave him the strength to do so.[7] As Fortin remarks, the difference between Augustine and many present-day thinkers lies in the fact "that Augustine was intent on preserving and restoring human wholeness by directing all of the individual's activities to the goal or goals to which they are intrinsically ordered."[8]

In this Augustine was putting in narrative form an intellectual ascent, the results of which can be found in many Greek and Latin Fathers. From Ambrose he had learned that presence precedes operation, so that all of history and time is present in God for God to work in history and time. He had heard that one is not to believe only what is seen with bodily eyes, for "what is not so seen is more truly seen, for what is [physically] seen belongs to time, but what is seen with the mind and soul belongs to eter-

---

6 St. Augustine, *Confessions* VII, 1.

7 Cf. St. Augustine, Confessions where, at the end of Book VIII he converts to Christ and how that enables him to live morally and intellectually. Thus, as Fortin remarks, we have the classic expression of the ascent to truth as God that Augustine has with his mother—to illustrate how the light of faith enables souls to enjoy a contemplation of the divine even if they lack formal intellectual training—in chapter 10 of Book IX.

8 Fortin, *The Birth of Philosophic Christianity*, 10.

nity."[9] The early Christian theologians joined classical philosophers in insisting that truth was normative for intelligence. Thus they often called their reflections, not *theologia*, a term linked with religious myths deceiving the many, but *philosophia*, the love of true wisdom.[10] Schoolmen, principally Thomas Aquinas, later articulated this distinction of intelligence and wisdom as truth in terms of the two sets of operations of the mind: understanding and judgment.[11]

Jewish and Christian revelation clearly distinguishes between God as infinite and creation as finite. God is the infinitely simple cause or ground or reason of all that is and occurs. God absolutely transcends the whole of creation. In Christian theology this led, in the thirteenth century, to a real distinction between the natural and the supernatural. This distinction involves a theory of the whole of nature as an ordered pattern of natures and events in the created universe, and how in those patterns what is higher sublates (without negating) what precedes it. Christian theology distinguished statements that draw upon what humans can naturally know about God, and other statements that are known only supernaturally, through faith. We are both creatures of God and called into intimate friendship with the Triune God. If faith is a knowledge born of this loving friendship, it is a knowing nonetheless. To know that God is and is the simple cause of all that is (metaphysics) and to know God as Triune friend (faith and theology) are both acts of knowing. Faith as a knowledge born of supernatural love is a healing elevation of our natural knowledge born of questioning. Neither grammar nor logic is adequate to understanding a discourse on God that attends to the horizons of those questioning and loving God: An ontology or metaphysics is needed for theological reflection.[12]

---

[9] Cf. Ambrose, *Tractatus de Mysteriis,* nos. 8–16. Note that for Ambrose, as for Augustine later, what is seen with the bodily eyes is real, but its reality is caused by what cannot be so seen, but only understood and judged by the mind. Presence *(praesentia)* refers to intelligent conscious self-presence. Mind is experienced as the highest form of presence.

[10] Cf. Robin Darling Young, "*Theologia* in the Early Church," *Communio* 24 (1997): 681–90.

[11] On Augustine, cf. Charles Boyer, SJ, *L'idée de vérité dans la philosophie de saint Augustin* (Paris: Beauchesne, 1920); on Aquinas, cf. Bernard Lonergan, SJ, *Verbum: Word and Idea in Aquinas,* ed. F. Crowe and R. Doran, (Toronto: University of Toronto Press, 1997), 3–105; and Frederick Crowe, SJ, *Three Thomist Studies* (Boston: Boston College Lonergan Institute, 2000).

[12] Cf. Ronald. H. Nash, *The Light of the Mind: St. Augustine's Theory of Knowledge* (Lexington, KY: University of Kentucky Press, 1969) and the somewhat critical

The type of knowing operative in metaphysics and in theology requires a normative grasp of knowing what we do when we know that we know. Conflicts and disagreements in metaphysics and in theology can be traced to failures to attain this normative grasp of the reality of knowing. What Bernard Lonergan sought to accomplish in his *Insight: A Study of Human Understanding* was to retrieve for contemporary intellectual seekers the intellectual conversion narrated in Plato's parable of the cave in the *Republic* and in Augustine's *Confessions*. In an essay titled "Natural Right and Historical Mindedness," Lonergan refers to Leo Strauss's work in support of how "underneath the manifold of human life-styles, there existed a component or factor that possessed the claims to universality and permanence of nature itself." But this component or factor admits of two very different interpretations. The first sees it as "universal propositions, self-evident truths, naturally known certitudes." In other words, it would substitute for nature abstract conceptions, as if there were only one set of acts of the mind summed up as thinking. But the other interpretation is of Strauss's return is to "nature, not as abstractly conceived, but as concretely operating." This is nature, as Aristotle defined it, as an immanent principle of movement and rest. The nature of the intelligent and rational soul is such that it raises and answers questions.[13]

Intelligence as such is infinite. Created intelligence is infinite in its potentiality, always finite in its achievements. Created intelligence is potentiality for the infinite, and this is experienced in the relentless drive of questions. The human race will never run out of questions, as we may run out of material resources such as oil or coal. For every question correctly answered more questions follow.[14]

Intelligence is thus normative precisely because it is marked by an ongoing openness to all further questions. The openness is never an indifference to contradictions, for then intelligence itself would cease. There would be no difference between an open mind and a closed mind, for

---

review by Fortin in *The Birth of Philosophic Christianity*, 314–17. Note that neither Nash, nor those he criticizes, analyzed sufficiently the distinctions Augustine draws between understanding and judging, conception and truth, cf. S. Biolo, *La coscienza nel 'De Trinitate' di S. Agostino* (Rome: Gregorian University Press, 1969).

13 Bernard Lonergan, *A Third Collection: Papers by Bernard J. F. Lonergan, SJ*, ed. Frederick Crowe (New York: Paulist Press, 1985), 172.

14 Cf. B. Lonergan on self-knowledge of the soul and the unity of wisdom in *Verbum*, 87–104.

mind itself would not be minded.[15] Besides the intelligibility informing all beings, there is the profounder intelligibility that is also intelligent. The vast expanses of space and time in the entire material universe, and the manifold intelligibilities constituting the ontological perfection of the ordered relationships as one moves from physics through chemistry and botany to zoology, do not account for the emergence of mind, of an intelligibility that is itself intelligent.[16]

There is an unlimited openness to questions that seek and demand correct answers. Nothing less than correct answers realize the potentiality of the questions. Infinity in the realm of intelligence is far different from infinity in the realm of quantity or of matter. For in intelligence the infinity of questions is not so much acted upon as itself active. It is an intelligible and intelligent desire and love for answers. It is a desiring love for meaning, intelligibility, and truth that will only reach fulfillment when it truly understands and knows. The norm is not in the answer but in the desiring question. The answer may be partial and incomplete, it may even be wrong, but the partiality, incompleteness, or falsehood will be discovered by the ongoing questioning desire. This *eros* of intelligence for intelligibility and truth is its nature as *imago Dei*.[17]

What is proportionate, therefore, to the infinity of the questioning is an act that is itself infinite. Only when we understand everything that there is to understand will the normative questioning desire be completely fulfilled. Only when the answer is the infinitely active Answer who is God will the normative character of the active questioning be properly fulfilled in transcending itself. The infinity of questions is possible only as created

---

[15] This is a key element in the ongoing tension between reason and revelation, Athens and Jerusalem, cf. Fortin, *The Birth of Philosophic Christianity*, 123–208 and his "Rational Theologians and Irrational Philosophers: A Straussian Perspective" and his favorable review of Robert Sokolowski's *The God of Faith and Reason in Classical Christianity and the Political Order*, 287–316.

[16] Note the crucial discovery of Augustine that while his mind generated endless images, it was not itself an image but a spiritual presence or light, *Confessions* VII, 1–13. So Lonergan remarks on the referent of Augustine's discovery and how this referent is a gradual realization that the real is not the same as body, something now realized after four centuries of developments in the natural sciences, cf. his *Insight: A Study of Human Understanding* (Toronto: University of Toronto Press, 1992), 15ff.

[17] For Augustine and Aquinas on this, cf. D. Juvenal Merriell, *To The Image of the Trinity: A Study in the Development of Aquinas' Teaching* (Toronto: Pontifical Institute of Medieval Studies, 1990).

intelligence oriented into, and completely dependent upon, the Infinite Knowing that is God. In questioning the very activity of our questioning, we arrive at the point where cognitional theory and metaphysics enters the specifically religious realm.

When we question our own activity of questioning, when our intelligence is heightened into a questioning of its own nature, then that very act of questioning is the key to the analogy of conceiving God as an infinite act of knowing and loving. For it is our conscious intelligence in act that is the natural created (and so finitely active) participation in the Infinite Act of Divine Intelligence. Attention should be directed toward the questioning since it is our questioning that is infinite potentiality. Each and every insight, understanding, judgment that occurs in us is finite, and so a certain "suffering" or *pati* occurs because those acts do not actualize the native infinity of intelligence as such, the infinite range or scope of our questioning mind. The answers are acknowledged as limited and finite because of the further relevant questions that spontaneously occur in our active intelligence.[18]

Aquinas analyzes in detail how the light of active intelligence illumines the human imagination, grasping the intelligibility in the phantasm *(species qua)* and understanding the universal in the particular *(species quae)*, then intelligently formulating the universal common to many in the concept *(species in qua)*. The intelligible is not known through "looking" with the senses. All the senses give the mind is data to be understood. It is the light of active intelligence that grasps the intelligible and so the universal in the particular. There is no antinomy between the universal and the particular, no contradiction between the singular and the species and genus to which it belongs. Aquinas states how by that light of active intelligence we can know truly and unchangeably very changeable and contingent things and events.[19]

The limitation of each answer is known in correct judgments, and we know that our judgments are correct, that we have weighed the evidence sufficiently, because the further relevant questions presuppose those judg-

---

[18] The infinity of questions, the *potens omnia fieri et facere* of the active intelligence or *intellectus agens* is a certain participation in divine intelligence, cf. Lonergan, *Verbum*, 78–103. For Aquinas on our intelligence consciousness is a created participation of the divine eternal light, cf. *Summa theologiae* I, q. 84, a. 5.

[19] Cf. *ST* I, q. 84, a. 6, ad 1: "For the light of agent intellect is needed by which we can know unchangeable truth in changeable things, and distinguish the things themselves from the [sensible] likenesses of things." For many other texts on how this light is operative in judging correctly, cf. Lonergan, *Verbum*, 90–103.

ments. The differentiation of understanding and knowing is crucial, for it is only when that differentiation is known that the infinity of intelligent desire to understand is properly related with the finitude of all created and concrete correct answers. The notion of being is not merely a conceptual content, a meaningful and intelligible idea. The notion of being is as universal and as concrete, as unrestricted and as spontaneous, as the infinite desire to know. While being is known in judgment, the notion of being precedes and underpins all human experience, understanding, and judging, deciding, and acting.[20]

Human intelligence as knowing is the best analogue to aid our understanding of God. There are no questions in God, only the infinite fullness of active intelligence. Divine Intelligence does not "suffer" the way created intelligence suffers. There are no further relevant questions unanswered by Infinite Divine Understanding. There is no "passivity" or "potentiality" in God. God is pure, infinite Act. Because Divine Intelligence is infinite actual understanding, Divine Love is pure enjoyment. There is no desire unrequited by Divine Love. Just as human intelligence presupposes the objects of its questioning, so human loving presupposes the objects of its desire. God presupposes nothing. Divine Intelligence and Love is utterly self-sufficient, and only because of this transcendent self-sufficiency freely creates everything.

Divine Eternity Creates Time

As God is simple, infinite understanding and loving, so God is eternal. There is no extension or duration in God. This divine eternity, as divine infinity and simplicity, cannot be imagined; nor can it be understood and conceived, except by God. We can, however, affirm that God is eternal and understand analogically that affirmation. There are major breakthroughs in the philosophical and theological grasp of this analogical understanding of the affirmation that God is eternal. Those breakthroughs are in the works of Augustine, Boethius, and Thomas Aquinas. Unfortunately, subsequent philosophers and theologians did not measure up to their achievements in this issue. A contrast with the greatest philosophers on this theme might bring out their achievement.

Divine eternity was not adequately understood without the context of revealed religion. In Greek and Roman cultures there were those rare

---

[20] Cf. Lonergan, *Insight,* 372–98.

philosophical achievements that recognized that the truly divine transcended change and multiplicity. There could not be more than one infinite Being, and this Being was both immutable and simple. Plato would
insist upon the absolute intelligibility of the eternal separating it from the
temporal. Aristotle would acknowledge a divine νοήσίς νοήσεως *[noêsis
noêseôs]* as eternal unmoved mover of the whole and so would seek to
ascribe some aspect of eternity to the concrete whole of the universe.

Without a clear attainment of judgment as affirming and denying
being, as a positing of the synthesis of subject and predicate, the efforts of
philosophers and theologians to understand the divine either made the
divine into Absolute Idea, the transcendence of which is its separation
from all finite beings; or they made the divine into an Absolute Intelligence that somehow informs the whole universe, immanent in all that is.

Parmenides and Zeno, in acknowledging the "all at once" character of
the one, argued against the reality of change. In Plato the divine eternal is
a unity beyond, and in opposition to, all multiplicity. In Aristotle the
divine eternal is the νοήσίς νοήσεως *[noêsis noêseôs]* as the immanent
unmoved mover of all that is. Where Plato can contrast the eternal and the
temporal to the point of opposing them, Aristotelian scholarship has been
unable to determine if the master ever decisively differentiated the eternal
and temporal. This has been a philosophical dialectic ever since: transcendence without immanence or immanence with a very questionable transcendence. This dialectic could be resolved only by adverting to what is
implied in the activity of judging, of knowing the truth, as distinct from
understanding and thinking. Neither Plato nor Aristotle it seems understood the act of judgment as more than the synthesis of concepts, of subject and predicate. Hence the notion of being was in some way a conceptual
content, an essence, without distinguishing that from existence or *esse*.
This distinction would result from adverting to judging as a positing of
the synthesis. The positing of the synthesis would have led, as it did in
Arab and Christian philosophers, to grasping a real distinction between
essence and existence.[21]

Perhaps the apogee of philosophical speculation on a divine eternity is
attained in the seventh chapter of Plotinus's *Third Ennead.* The divine eter-

---

21 Cf. E. Gilson, *Being and Some Philosophers,* second corrected edition (Toronto:
PIMS, 1952); C. Fabro, *Participation et causalité selon S. Thomas D'Aquin* (Louvain: Publications Universitaires de Louvain, 1961); Rudi A. te Velde, *Participation and Substantiality in Thomas Aquinas* (Leiden: E. J. Brill, 1995).

nal selfsame is the whole as present without extension or duration. This is contrasted with the mutability of time. Similar to Plato and Aristotle, Plotinus could only treat judgment as a synthesis of subjects and predicates, so that the notion of being was a conceptual content to be known by a direct act of understanding ἐννοεῖν *[hennoeîn]* rather than by the indirect way of analogically understanding that we know in judgment. The divine eternal being is that which "always exists" beyond all extension and duration. The eternal and the temporal are opposites, and the task of the true philosopher or mystic is to leave behind all the temporal for the super-intuition of the eternal. Eternity is "intelligible nature" φύσις νοητική *[physis noêtikê]* that is contrasted with and transcends time, which is identified as the whole order of the heavens and earth. The antithesis of understanding and what is understood is heightened into the antithesis of the eternal and the temporal. Plotinus did not overcome but only intensified the contrast between the eternal and the temporal in Plato.[22]

To understand eternity required both an appropriation of intelligence as not intrinsically conditioned by space or time, and a grasp of the concreteness of being known by judgment. Only if these came together would there be the proper analogue for understanding God as the eternal creating the temporal. The revelation of God's covenant with Israel, and the universality of the new covenant in the life, death, and resurrection of Jesus Christ, evoked both differentiations. The judgments of faith were affirmations of a Loving God acting in history, judgments inspired by supernatural faith and so called forth an ongoing effort to understand, however imperfectly and analogically. The pedagogy of the Jewish Scriptures reveals an ever-deepening understanding of God from the tribal through the liberating warrior and the protector of the nation to the mysteriously transcendent God of the prophets and wisdom literature. The transcendent God is immanent in the messianic suffering of Israel. This process of graced differentiation included both serene contemplation and the intense and passionate questioning of itself and God in psalm, prayer, sacrifice, and suffering—the entire concrete history of a people covenanted with the mysterious and loving God.

---

[22] Cf. Pierre Hadot, *Plotinus and the Simplicity of Vision*, trans. Michael Chase (Chicago: University of Chicago Press, 1993). On the consequences for political philosophy, see Fortin, *The Birth of Philosophic Christianity*, 181–87. For a fine outline of Augustine's reflections on God, see Lewis Ayres and Michel R. Barnes's article on "God" in Alan D. Fitzgerald, ed., *Augustine Through the Ages: An Encyclopedia* (Grand Rapids, MI: Eerdmans, 1999), 384–90.

The incarnation of the Word in Jesus Christ revealed God's absolutely supernatural and definitive redemption of the human race, not by removing evil and sin through power, but by transforming evil into good through the life, death, and resurrection of Jesus. The covenant is now friendship with God the Father through incorporation into Christ and the gift of God's own Love flooding human hearts by the Holy Spirit. The temporal manifestation of the Triune God's redemptive presence in the words and deeds of Jesus Christ became the outer words—living on in church, Scripture, and sacrament—which can only be recognized as true in the light of faith. The true judgments of faith are grounded in the graced real presence of the Triune God elevating human knowing and loving into a participation of their own Infinite Understanding generating Infinite Truth spirating Infinite Love. In the incarnation of the Word, who enlightens every human being coming into this world, the eternal is incarnate in the temporal. Triune absolute transcendence is invisibly and visibly immanent in human history. The visible mediations indicate how the word of God as true is conditioned by history. Christian theologians were challenged to go beyond the antinomies of Platonic and Aristotelian conceptions of the eternal and temporal.

Augustine initiated a major breakthrough. His own discovery of intelligence was marked by both the Platonic concern for the spiritual nature of human intelligence and the Christian insistence upon the word of God as known in true judgments of faith. The light of reason and the light of faith both come together in the life praxis of intellectual, moral, and religious conversion narrated in books five through nine of his *Confessions*.[23] For Augustine the graced turning to divine revelation enabled him to understand the intrinsic goodness of the whole of creation. Evil results only from the free disordered acts of intelligent creatures rejecting divine friendship. Both faith and reason prompted Augustine to inquire into the wonders of the world and human nature in order to understand the wonders of God's creative and redemptive presence. In his writings Augustine narrates the ongoing mutual self-mediations of Jesus Christ and Christians constituting the church in the kingdom or city of God, who, in their

---

[23] On philosophy as a way of life, a spiritual exercise or praxis of theoretical reflection on wisdom, cf. Pierre Hadot, *Philosophy as a Way of Life,* trans. Michael Case (Oxford: Blackwell, 1995); on the confluence of knowing and loving in Augustine, cf. Fortin's "Augustine and the Hermeneutics of Love" in *The Birth of Philosophic Christianity.*

many conscious acts and decisions, are in conversation with the Triune God who is more intimate to each of us than we are even to ourselves.[24]

Augustine's inquiry into the nature of intelligence is always in the interpersonal context of this ongoing mutual self-mediation of his friendship with God. The analogue for understanding God's eternal present is the intelligent human experience of knowing that I know myself to be now present to myself. The movement of time does not intrinsically condition or constitute who I am, for the past exists only in my present memory, and the future exists only in my present expectation.

To understand Augustine's notion of human and divine presence, it is necessary to undergo the process of intellectual, moral, and religious conversion that he narrates. There is needed, therefore, a dialectical discernment whereby Augustine's achievement is not simply reduced to textual comparisons. He has left records of his very concrete sufferings and struggles, and they should not be made paper-thin by treating them as texts without references to a very real way of living. A major criterion for the intellectual aspect of Augustine's ongoing conversions is his overcoming the limitations of materialism and its naive realism. It would be a mistake, in my judgment, to reduce this intellectual way of life, and the conversion to mind, to no more than a career change that "everyone could understand."[25]

By adverting to the nature of intelligently knowing the truth, Augustine was able to bring together the eternal divine presence and the totality of time in all its concrete universality. Eternity does not denigrate time, but creates time in order, through intelligent creatures, to invite a return. Augustine presents God as *totum esse praesens*, the fullness of Being as Presence freely creating, sustaining, and redeeming the universe and all of human history in the Triune Presence. All extensions and durations, all past, present, and future events, are present in the immutable and eternal

---

24 Cf. M. Lamb, "Divine Transcendence and Eternity," in Anthony J. Cernera, ed., *Continuity and Plurality in Catholic Theology* (Fairfield, CT: Sacred Heart University Press, 1998), 77–106; as well as chapter 1 above.

25 This is the approach in Peter Brown, *Augustine of Hippo: A Biography* (Berkeley: University of California Press, 1967), 101–14. Brown writes on 101: "Augustine's reading of the Platonic books had done one thing which everyone could understand: they had brought Augustine to a final and definitive 'conversion' from a literary career to a life 'in Philosophy.'" This tends to reduce intellectual conversion to no more than a career change. It is unfortunate that so influential a biography could miss the depths of what was so central to Augustine's life. Only those who similarly undergo an intellectual conversion can understand what it means. Note Fortin's similar criticism of the biography in *The Birth of Philosophic Christianity*, 307–9.

understanding, knowing, and loving who are Father, Word, and Spirit. The eternal God creates the universe in the totality of its spatiotemporal reality. There is no before or after in God's eternal presence.[26]

Boethius carried forward Augustine's breakthrough both by providing philosophical precision, and by indicating how a correct analogue sublates the positions of Plato and Aristotle. There is the immanence of the whole of the created spatiotemporal universe in the absolute transcendence of God's knowing presence:

> That God is eternal is the common judgment of all who live by reason. We shall therefore reflect on what is eternity since this makes evident the divine nature as well as divine knowledge. Eternity is the whole, simultaneous and perfect possession of limitless life. . . . Since then every judgment comprehends those things subject to it according to its own nature, and God has an always eternal and present nature, then his knowledge too, surpassing all movement of time, is permanent in the simplicity of his present, and embracing all the infinite spaces of the future and the past, considers them in his simple act of knowledge as though they were now going on. So if you should wish to consider his foreknowledge, by which he discerns all things, you will more rightly judge it to be not foreknowledge as it were of the future but knowledge of a never-passing instant.[27]

Thomas Aquinas placed the teachings of Augustine and Boethius on the eternity of God in the systematic framework of discourse on God. When it comes to the divine, it is not our acts of understanding on which we must rely so much as on our acts of judging. In this life we do not know *what* God is (essence and meaning defined in relation to acts of understanding) but *that* God is (existence and fact defined in relation to acts of judgment). Anselm's proof for the existence of God was not adequate because it had failed to articulate this context of judgment in our knowledge of God. The proofs for the existence of God that Aquinas gives are all indicative of how only God is the complete and satisfying answer that, when known, would leave no further questions to be asked. The fact of correct judgments regarding motion, efficient causality, necessity and possibility, scales of perfection, and finality all indicate that judgments of

---

26 Cf. Augustine, *Confessions* XI, 10–13; also Frederick Crowe, "Rethinking Eternal Life" in *Science et Esprit* 45(1 and 2; January–May 1993): 25–39 and 145–59.

27 Boethius, *Philosophiae Consolationis* V, 6 [my translation].

fact and of goodness or value presuppose, by the very unlimited character of our desire to know, that God exists as the infinitely perfect and fully intelligent Being ultimately grounding all correct finite judgments. Because we know God in correct judgments of reason and of faith, we can by reflection on the light by which we make those judgments know what God is not and so remove all limitations from our knowledge of God.[28]

Besides the systematic context of judgment, Aquinas also attended to the nature of intelligence as the immaterial image of God. Like Boethius he sought to show how a Christian theology of the eternal God sublates the positions of Plato and Aristotle. In *Summa contra Gentiles* much use is made of Aristotle in the proofs for *Deum esse*, how we know God *via remotionis* (I, ch. 14), then a series of chapters dealing with how God transcends all finite beings, beginning with God as eternal and ending with divine simplicity and perfection (I, chs. 15–28). In *Summa theologiae* the order is reversed, indicating how the simplicity, perfection, and goodness of God leads to the divine presence immanent in all being, and ending with God as immutable and eternal (*ST* I, qq. 3–11). Aquinas clearly states that "not only is God eternal, but God is his eternity."[29] Only God is eternity as the fullness of being *(esse)* or life totally present. God's ubiquitous presence is really the presence of all finite existence in the creative act of God, which act is identical with God's own being. Because God is pure being *(esse)*, understanding *(intelligere)*, and loving *(amare)*, the creative act is a supremely free act, since God in no way depends on creatures while all of creation depends utterly on God. Since eternity is identified most properly with God, so too is time identified most properly with material creation.[30] Aquinas, having achieved the intellectual conversion

---

28 The distinction of the two operations of intelligence, and the centrality of judgment as analogue for understanding something of God, is usually overlooked by those who fail to see the profound differences between analogies depending upon the spiritual nature of intelligence and metaphors draw from sense experience. The *via negativa* in analogy denies the limitations of our knowledge of being, goodness, truth, beauty, etc. When it comes to sensible metaphors (e.g., God is a rock) the negation is of the sensible thing itself, not just of its limitations.

29 *ST* I, q. 10, a. 2.

30 Cf. Brian J. Shanley, OP, "Eternity and Duration in Aquinas," *The Thomist* 61 (1997): 525–48. The "eternity of the world"—what is sometimes called its "sempiternity"—is not a problem for Aquinas since it clearly is not *tota simul.* Even unending temporality would not have the total presence of all times and being in the total simultaneity of Divine Presence.

narrated by Augustine, was fond of calling attention to the hypothetical necessity of true judgments about all contingent free events:

> Divine foreknowledge does not impose necessity on things . . . by reason of the correspondence with the thing known—which correspondence is required by the notion of truth and the certainty of knowledge—because that correspondence of God's knowledge with the thing is relevant, not as the thing exists in its causes, in which case it exists as a possible future only, but in relation to the thing itself inasmuch as it has determinate being as present and not future.[31]

God's eternal presence is knowable by created intelligence (*ST* I, q. 12), for created minds can know God since there is a natural desire in all created intellects to ask what something is once it is known that it is. But only the absolutely supernatural light of agapic love and of glory will enable us to know God as God is (*ST* I, q. 12, a. 5). Moreover, since this is in proportion to our desire, the greater the agapic love or desire is, the more fully God will be known as God is (*ST* I, q. 12, a. 6). The ascent of the mind to God is clearly a series of sublations from the light of reason, through the light of faith and agapic love, to the light of glory. The higher in no way negate but only elevate the lower. To affirm the eternal God as Aquinas did requires the systematic context of a differentiated self-knowledge and the role of judgment as a created participation in divine intelligent consciousness or light.[32] Aquinas then proceeded to transform Aristotle's teaching on friendship in order to show how caritas as a supernatural love natural only to God himself enables those on whom God bestows it to strengthen, heal, and elevate their human erotic love and their friendships.[33]

---

[31] Thomas Aquinas, *Super I Sententiarum,* d. 40, q. 3, a. 1. This line of argument, as Lonergan remarks, runs throughout Aquinas's writings. Cf. Brian Shanley, OP, "Eternal Knowledge of the Temporal in Aquinas," *American Catholic Philosophical Quarterly* 71 (1977): 1–28.

[32] On the theoretic transposition of the "light of the mind" and judgment in Aquinas, cf. Lonergan, *Verbum,* 87–104; and Frederick Crowe, "Universal Norms and the Concrete *Operabile* in St. Thomas Aquinas" in his *Three Thomist Studies,* 1–70.

[33] Notice how Thomas Aquinas carefully comments on Aristotle's eighth book of the *Nicomachean Ethics,* staying close to the text, compared with his analysis of charity in *ST* II–II, qq. 23–46.

Misunderstandings: Later Medieval and Modern

John Duns Scotus had a far greater influence on subsequent philosophical and theological thought than Thomas Aquinas. Scotus flatly denied apprehensive abstraction as insight into phantasm.[34] For Scotus concepts come first, then the mind apprehends nexi between concepts; external words immediately reference intelligible species that exist because knowing presupposes its object as present. The first act of the mind is the production of intelligible species by agent intellect and the phantasm; the second act is an inner word that is intuitive or abstractive knowing.[35] Thus Bernard Lonergan comments:

> The Scotist rejection of insight into phantasm necessarily reduced the act of understanding to seeing a nexus between concepts; hence, while for Aquinas understanding precedes conceptualization which is rational, for Scotus understanding is preceded by conceptualization which is a matter of metaphysical mechanics. It is the latter position that gave Kant the analytic judgments which he criticized; and it is the real insufficiency of that position which led Kant to assert his synthetic a priori judgments. . . . [Kant's] critique was not of the pure reason but of the human mind as conceived by Scotus.[36]

Without an adequate notion of judgment as analogue, Scotus's notion of eternity and time relied upon the divine will more than divine intelligence. Divine infinity and divine free will are prologues to later discussions of divine power and, in Ockham, a scholastic agnosticism linked with voluntarism.[37] A perceptualistic and logistic matrix replaced the non-imaginable but highly intelligible matrix of the theory of divine eternity in Augustine, Boethius, and Aquinas. Perceptualism, conceptualism, and later voluntarism contended for dominance. Nominalism assured the triumph of logical analysis over genuinely ontological or metaphysical analysis. Augustinians emphasized the

---

[34] John Duns Scotus, *Opera Omnia,* vol. IX, *Quaestiones in Librum Primum Sententiarum* (Paris: Vivès, 1893) d. 3, q. 6, 10–12, pp. 250–51. For a comparison and contrast between Aquinas and Scotus, cf. Michel Bastit, *Les principes des choses en ontologie médiévale: Thomas d'Aquin, Scot, Occam* (Bordeaux : Editions Bière, 1997).

[35] Ibid., vol. I: *De Modis Significandi* (Paris: Vivès, 1896), q. 2, 3, p. 541; vol. IX, d. 3, q. 4, 7–8, pp. 173–76; q. 6, 5–14, pp. 236–55; q. 7, 15, pp. 543–44; q. 7, 21–22, pp. 362–63.

[36] Cf. Lonergan, *Verbum,* 38–39.

[37] Cf. Fortin, *The Birth of Philosophic Christianity,* 242–43.

absolute transcendence of God, and the need for spiritual ascent through love to God. Less attention was paid to Augustine's affirmations of knowing that we know (judgment), so that when Descartes's *cogito ergo sum* was enunciated most could not distinguish thinking from knowing, and eternity was increasingly defined as a simple and total negation of time. Thomists opposed Cartesian thinking with the dependence of the mind on sensations, perceptions, and images. But not attending to the light of active intelligence and the objective abstraction of the *species qua* there was a tendency to link the empirical with the conceptual, and observations with logic, in ways that would eventuate into the perennial modern dichotomies of empiricism versus idealism. Divine immutability was imagined as an absolute concept or idea, rather than as the fullness of being, understanding, and loving. Universals could not be concrete but only nominal, as metaphysics and theology was farmed out to the grammarians and logicians.[38]

The stage was set for Spinoza's claim that any transcendence of nature was a contradiction of nature. Not only is God eternal and infinite, but also all that flows from God is eternal and infinite, so that eternity becomes a *natura naturans* of unlimited duration. A genuine theology of the supernatural was lost in a *deus sive natura*. The genuine character of judgment was eclipsed, with the result that mysticism retreated into a private arcanum and faith was deemed to be arational or irrational. The emergence of the empirical sciences and historical consciousness initially solidified this eclipse of judgment, for knowledge was limited to what can be verified by appeals to sensible data.

Lessing's comment that "accidental truths of history can never become the proof of necessary truths of reason" highlighted the opposition between the historical particularities of revealed religions as opposed to the rigorous conceptualism of rationalism. The opposition between the eternal and the temporal flowed from and into an opposition between the universal and the particular. Rousseau's *Confessions*, for example, set the framework for a notion of self that is radically truncated by the accidents of space and time. Unlike Augustine's *Confessions*, which are animated by intelligence in conversation with God, Rousseau's autobiography is an egophanic litany of specific dates and places betokening a contraction of

---

[38] On the misunderstandings of Aquinas in nominalism, cf. Edward P. Mahoney, ed., *Thomas Aquinas and Gabriel Biel: Interpretations of Thomas Aquinas in German Nominalism on the Eve of the Reformation* (Durham: Duke University Press, 1988).

consciousness, one that abandons the dynamism of self-presence for the monadism of self-regard.[39] Finally, the early Heidegger thoroughly appropriated the Scotistic derailment on being as concept and the logistic dominance of metaphysical or ontological thinking.[40]

Theology either hardened into a fundamentalism/dogmatism or shifted from truth to meaning, as biblical exegetes uncovered the multiple meanings of scriptural texts and historians grappled with the many texts and events constitutive of Christian history. Which meanings were "more meaningful" depended upon which set of categories seemed more plausible, with a succession of conceptual contenders. The discerning functions of dialectics were ignored as foundations meant commitments to one or another set of meanings and moral theology or ethics was either casuist or voluntaristic. While meaning is sought after, and commitment called for, the truth of judgment is left to the vagaries of power. It is exceedingly difficult, as the works of Michel Foucault demonstrate, for moderns to distinguish truth from power. This is especially so for religious truths. The European wars of religion led to an Enlightenment that would critique revealed religion as bellicose while it proclaimed war as intrinsic to human nature.

To a modern mind, steeped in historicism, both reason and faith are truncated and constricted. The doctrines of faith seem to be empty statements at best to be interpreted as "symbols," "metaphors," "myths," or "ciphers" of some unknowable and unknown mystery. Lost to such a mind is the realization that doctrines express true realities, that the affirmations of faith are confessions of the realities of God's creative and redemptive presence. While modern theology would exalt religious experience, it would

---

[39] As Rousseau writes: "My purpose is to display to my kind a portrait in every way true to nature, and the man I shall portray will be myself. Simply myself . . . I am made unlike any one I have ever met; I will even venture to say that I am like no one in the whole world. I may be no better, but at least I am different. Whether Nature did well or ill in breaking the mould in which she formed me, is a question which can only be resolved after the reading of my book." Rousseau concludes his *Confessions* with the very egophanic assertion that if anyone disagrees that he is an honorable man, he ought to be "stifled."

[40] Martin Heidegger, *Die Kategorien- und Bedeutungslehre des Duns Scotus* (Tübingen: Verlag von JCB Mohr, 1916); John Van Buren points out how the young Heidegger used "pure logic" in his exploration of the categories in Duns Scotus, cf. his *The Young Heidegger: Rumor of the Hidden King* (Bloomington: Indiana University Press, 1994), 51–64; on the way this led to a logicistic conception of judgment, ibid., 65–86. This casts a different light on the quote from Strauss on Heidegger and Aquinas at the beginning of Merrill's essay, cf. note 3 above.

also confine such experience within the narrow limits of a conceptualism innocent of judgment. Meaning, cut off from judgment, is unable to raise the question of truth, and is left instead merely to disclose varieties of possibilities. Among these different meanings, like shoppers in a mall, one is left to choose those to which one will be "committed." Go to the church and/or doctrine of your choice. The trouble is that such commitment, severed from judgment, becomes merely "voluntary" and "arbitrary." So, in the end, power dominates and truth is silenced. Ecumenism in some circles aspires only to tolerance, and religious indifferentism spreads.[41]

Return to the Eternal

To reach up to the mind of an Augustine, Boethius, or Aquinas involves a realization that human intelligence is not intrinsically conditioned by space and time. There is the fact that once correct understanding occurs, the place and time of its occurrence do not enter into the act of correct understanding itself: We do not have to return to our study in order to understand what we grasped last night in that study. If intelligence were intrinsically conditioned by space and time, then we would need different sciences and scholarships for different places and times. There would be one chemistry for France and another for England. Moreover, the difference intelligence makes for the human species is decisive, for it is not so much a higher system in the grades of being, but a recurrent source of higher systems. If species are solutions to problems of living, then the human species, thanks to intelligence, need not change its species with new sciences, civilizations, philosophies, or theologies.

A return to the eternal is a return home to intelligence. Just as the light of faith enabled Christian philosophers and theologians to acknowledge Divine Being and Divine Infinite Intelligence as Father, Son, and Spirit, so too did that same light enable them to envisage the return to the eternal as a return to God's infinite love. Far from denigrating creation and the natural universe, the eternal God loves the entire universe in all its spatiotemporal detail into its existence and its return to Himself. This is the *exitus–reditus* theme in which Aquinas structured his *Summa theologiae*. Because human intelligence is not intrinsically conditioned by space and time, the gifted

---

41 Cf. Fortin, "Nietzsche and the Crisis of Nihilism," in *Classical Christianity and the Political Order*, 337–53.

light of faith, as well as the light of glory in the beatific vision of God in no way negate the natural light of intelligence that they heal and elevate.[42]

That our intelligence is extrinsically conditioned by space and time is evident in the long process of questioning, of coming to understand, of verifying our hypotheses. Human intelligence develops, not only in our individual lives, but also throughout the course of human history. Knowing provides an analogical understanding of God as eternal in such a way that divine eternity does not negate but creates the totality of time, including all of human history in such a way that human freedom is not denied but affirmed. We have sketched how Augustine, Boethius, and Aquinas provide a systematic context for this analogical understanding. Correct judgments, even of particular and concrete events, transcend the time and place of their utterance. History with all its contingent events is not historicist. Objective knowledge is attained each and every time correct judgments are made. The presence of truth is not hidden, lost among shadow movements of a thinking closed in on itself. Judgment is a reasoned act, not an arbitrary decision cutting off further reflection.

Bernard Lonergan, on the basis of his retrieval of Aquinas, developed an analogy drawn from a natural knowledge of God. This analogy, properly understood and developed, would check the tendencies in modern cultures to either treat religious discourse as utilitarian, or to dismiss it as fanatical fundamentalism. God, Divine Being as Presence, creates and embraces the concrete totality and universality of all created beings in all of their multiple acts whether natural or free. There is no time in God's own being, and so in this sense God is timeless. But God's eternal presence creates everything that is, so that all of time is present in God. Time is only by, with, and in eternity—as creation is only by, with, and in God. God created the universe, not some emanation from God. God redeems us, not some created emanation from God. Graced friendship with God is with God, not with some created emanation of God.[43]

The issue of divine foreknowledge is solved by extrapolating from the analysis of Aquinas:

---

[42] Cf. Lonergan, *Verbum,* 90–103; *Insight,* 343–71; Michael Miller, "Transcendence and Divine Causality," *American Catholic Philosophical Quarterly* 73 (1999): 537–54; Germaine Cromp, *Les sources de l'abstraction de l'intellect agent and her L'intellect agent et son rôle d'abstraction* (Montreal: University of Montreal, 1980).

[43] Cf. J. Michael Stebbins, *The Divine Initiative: Grace, World-Order, and Human Freedom in the Early Writings of Bernard Lonergan* (Toronto: University of Toronto Press, 1995), 212–76.

If the future is known with certainty, then necessarily it must come to be; and what necessarily must come to be, is not contingent but necessary. But St. Thomas denies that God knows events as future. He is not in time but an eternal "now" to which everything is present. Hence, when you say, "If God knows this, this must be," the "this" of the apodosis must be taken in the same sense as the "this" of the protasis. But the "this" of the protasis is present; therefore, the "this" of the apodosis is present; it follows that "this must be" is not absolute but hypothetical necessity: "necesse . . . est Socratem currere dum currit."[44]

Are all of these operations attributed to God identical with God's eternal divine nature? Yes, for in God there is no real distinction of the divine being and divine action or operation. For the divine nature is a simple, single act "that at once is unrestricted understanding and perfect affirming and perfect loving; and it is identical with the primary intelligible and the primary truth and the primary good."[45]

Does all of human history, with all of its contingency and freedom, thereby get swallowed up in the Divine, necessary, eternal being? Not at all, for the analogy from a natural knowledge of God emphasizes how God's nature is pure, infinite intelligence in act. Intelligence in act can choose a contingent course of action attentively, intelligently, reasonably, and responsibly. Such attributes are not lacking in the infinite intelligence and love that is God. The entire *De Auxiliis* controversy, as well as the Enlightenment theodicy problematic, rests upon not only false, mechanistic misunderstandings of God's Being, but also, and closer to home, false and mechanistic misunderstandings of human reason and freedom.[46]

The Cartesian dualism between *res extensa* and *res cogitans*, between thinking ideas and extension-duration, led to a fixation upon what Hegel called the *Denkender Geist Gottes* as infinite power. Whether one was a nominalist-voluntarist and claimed arbitrary power for God, or a rationalist and claimed necessary power for God, the point was, as Hegel stated so forcefully, Reason is infinite power *(Macht)* to realize itself in history. The temporal and spatial takes on absolute proportions, so that, as Johann B. Metz has

---

44 Bernard Lonergan, *Grace and Freedom: Operative Grace in the Thought of St. Thomas Aquinas* (Toronto: University of Toronto Press, 2000), 107.

45 Cf. B. Lonergan, *Insight*, 682.

46 Cf. Stebbins, *The Divine Initiative*, 3–182. On the *De Auxiliis* controversy, cf. ibid., 183–211. On Enlightenment modernity, cf. Fortin, *Human Rights, Virtue, and the Common Good*, 135–58.

remarked, contemporary cultures seem caught in the endless continuum of a history in which transcendence is decapitated into an inescapable mechanistic and technological-material "progress" that has lost both freedom and wisdom. Hobbes illustrates this when he dismisses all reflection on an eternal-now as so much scholastic cant, only to embrace dominative power of the state (our "Mortal God") and fear-driven science in the war of all against all. Man, Freud later concluded, has become "a kind of prosthetic god."[47]

The analogy of a natural knowledge of God, attending as it does to true judgments, offers a wise alternative to such modern derailments. For it derives Divine Eternity, not from some absolutist arbitrary or voluntaristic power, but from the Divine Simplicity. For the truth of any contingent statement that from "all eternity"—a possibly misleading phrase since eternity is "all at once" *(tota simul)*—God understood and knew and loved such and such to happen is simply that such and such happens. What is required is not some physical premotion by which the Divine Engineer moves such and such to occur, nor some *scientia media*, some mid-range thinking, by which the Divine Bureaucrat knows how to stage things so such and such will occur. No, all that is required for the truth of the statement is for it to happen. God simply and eternally understands, knows, and loves everything good that occurs in human history.[48]

Redemption of Intellectual and Moral Excellence

What about the evil and suffering staining every day of human history? The analogy drawn from our natural knowledge of God confronts us with the limitations of our natural understanding, knowing, and loving. The gap between our essential freedom and our effective freedom is one that, if

---

[47] Johann B. Metz and Josef Cardinal Ratzinger, *Ende der Zeit? Die Provokation der Rede von Gott* (Mainz: Grünewald Verlag, 1999), 32–49. Thomas Hobbes, *Leviathan* (Indianapolis, IN: Hackett Publishing Company, 1994), 22–27, 109. Sigmund Freud, *Civilization and Its Discontents* (New York: W. W. Norton, 1961), 43.

[48] Cf. Lonergan, *Grace and Freedom*, 80–116. Lonergan's retrieval of Augustine and Aquinas enabled him to reject the modern dualism of sensing and thinking in favor of an attentive understanding, knowing, and responsible acting. So he developed, not an analogy of historical being as power, but an analogy of a natural knowledge of God as Unrestricted Understanding, Perfect Affirming, and Unconditional Loving. Intelligence, truth, and love are the analogues for our knowing the Divine Mystery. The analogy of natural knowledge of God, or of contingent predication, derives Divine Eternity from the Divine Simplicity.

we humans are on our own, will never be closed. A critically realist understanding of how humans actually live and treat one another would hardly inspire confidence in human intelligence and love. Indeed, modernity seemed to surrender to the counsel of despair, as its major minds conceded that power rather than understanding and love is the means of forcing reason and order on what Hegel termed the "butcher's block" of history.

Without the missions of the Son and Spirit, without a revelatory self-communication of God in history and the higher viewpoint provided by faith as a knowledge born of unconditional love (Romans 5:5), the social surds of history would set death and destruction as a dead-end to all human striving and living. The immense aspirations and efforts of countless human beings in acquiring skills, developing intellectual and moral virtues—the wisdom of a Socrates, Plato, Aristotle—all these noble and godlike achievements are not destined to end in death and obliteration. The eternal is no apersonal permanence; the eternal is inter-personal presence. The drama of human life is not confined to this mortal life. We are not alone as a human race. We are not cosmic orphans abandoned by the Light who created us. We are called into the Interpersonal Community of the Triune God, called to share with Christ in Infinite Understanding generating Infinite Truth spirating Infinite Love. An analogical understanding of eternity and time brings together both the analogy of being and the analogy of faith, both a metaphysics concerned with the proper understanding of the natural and a theology concerned with the mutual self-mediation of Divine and human persons knowing and loving each other in a city beyond all human imagination in its perfect justice, infinite goodness, and pure active intelligence. Far from denigrating the achievements of intellectual and moral excellence, a genuine retrieval of the theoretical transformations wrought by Augustine, Boethius, and Aquinas will contribute no small measure to an understanding of how the light of faith, hope, and agapic love redeem what is most noble, good, and true in human strivings for moral and intellectual excellence.[49]

The challenge facing philosophers and theologians today is twofold. First is the task of reaching up or returning to the truly great philosophers and theologians of the past in order to be transformed by the truth and

---

[49] Cf. Fortin, *The Birth of Philosophic Christianity,* 1–39, 209–50; Lonergan, *Insight,* 709–70; idem, *De Deo Trino,* vol. II: *Pars Systematica* (Rome: Gregorian University Press, 1964), 255–56.

wisdom they communicate. The second task is transposing that truth and wisdom to the manifold problems and issues of today. That such a monumental challenge is not impossible is illustrated in the life and teachings of Fr. Ernest Fortin.

CHAPTER 4

The Eschatology of
St. Thomas Aquinas

THE WHOLE OF THEOLOGY is profoundly eschatological according to St. Thomas Aquinas's *Summa theologiae*. Theology is a knowledge or science that is dependent on the knowledge of God and of the blessed in heaven for its principles.[1] This demonstrates the foundational importance of revelation and faith for the whole of theology, and with that the expectation of the human quest for understanding and the knowledge of faith flowering in the beatific knowledge of glory.

Aquinas's theological vision moves from the most sacred mystery of the Triune God to take in the cosmic sweep of the procession of all creation from God and the return of all to God. The end is in the beginning and the beginning in the end. The whole of reality and being is theologically viewed as coming from the Triune God and returning to a most intimate and intense interpersonal communion of knowing and loving the Father in the Son with the Holy Spirit.

Eschatology is the teleology of redeemed creation in the fullness of the Kingdom of God. This redemption of fallen creation is fulfilled in the visible and invisible missions of the Word Incarnate in Jesus Christ and by His Holy Spirit. The Church carries forward these missions in her sacramental worship with the preaching and teaching of the Apostles and their successors down the ages. The realities of the end or *telos* of all creation

---

This essay was originally published as "The Eschatology of St. Thomas Aquinas" in Thomas Weinandy, Daniel Keating, and John Yocum, eds. *Aquinas on Doctrine* (London: T&T Clark, 2004), 225–40.

[1] *Summa theologiae* I, q. 1, a. 2.

include: (1) its fulfillment in the eternal joy in the beatific Kingdom of God; (2) the resurrection of all humanity in Christ; and (3) Christ's judgment of the living and the dead, eternal punishment and eternal joy in the new heavens and the new earth.

The greatest contribution of Aquinas to eschatology is his profound analysis of beatitude as the fulfillment of the deepest desires of intelligent creatures and the whole of creation. He spelt out in careful cognitive and metaphysical terms the full implications of St. Augustine's "our hearts are restless until they rest in Thee."[2] Eternal beatitude in the beatific vision contextualizes Aquinas's eschatology within the orders of wisdom so fundamental to his entire systematic theology. Moreover, it was precisely the intellectually challenging analysis of the beatific vision in Aquinas that enabled him to show the intelligibility of the resurrection of the body and the telos of the whole material universe in the whole Christ.

Wisdom and Beatitude

In speaking of God creating, redeeming, becoming Incarnate, sending the Holy Spirit, beatifying the saints, and performing all the "great deeds of God" revealed in the Scriptures, it is important to observe what Aquinas calls "the order of wisdom." Divine Being is Infinite Act and Infinite Wisdom, so that "in God his operation is his substance; thus, as his substance is eternal, so is his action. But it does not follow that an operational effect is eternal, but that the effect is according to the order of wisdom, which is the principle of [divine] operation."[3] Divine Wisdom can be known by intelligent creatures in ever fuller ways according to how they participate in the Divine Wisdom or Divine Light. Indeed, the Divine Wisdom is the Triune God knowing and loving himself as Father, Son, and Holy Spirit, and knowing and loving all else into being as finite participations of the Divine Trinitarian being. All created beings do not exist by themselves but receive their being and existence from God.

---

2 St. Augustine, *Confessions* I, 1. See also Jean-Pierre Torrell, OP, *Saint Thomas d'Aquin, maître spirituel* (Fribourg: Editions Universitaires de Fribourg, 1996), 456–69.

3 Cf. *Super I Sententiarum* d. 8, q. 3, a. 1 ad 4: "In Deo autem operatio sua est sua substantia: unde sicut substantia est aeterna, ita et operatio. Sed non sequitur operationem operatum ab aeterno, sed secundum ordinem sapientiae, quae est principium operandi." Also, ibid., d. 35, q. 1, a. 5 ad 3; *De veritate* 23, 2; *De potentia* 1, 1 ad 8.

From late medieval nominalism and voluntarism, moderns are used to reading the creative and redemptive action of God as an expression of his power and will, rather than as an expression of his wisdom. Wisdom attunes the mind to the whole of reality, to the whole pattern in which all the parts can be understood as reaching their full purpose and nature. Wisdom discerns the patterns and ends of each in relation to the end of the whole.[4] Aquinas developed what might be termed wisdom eschatology, discerning the ordering patterns of fulfillment of creation and redemption in the eternal kingdom of God.

Such a wisdom or sapiential eschatology stresses the wholeness of the divine wisdom in creation and redemption, as well as continuity with Patristic eschatologies.[5] This is very different from the post-Enlightenment efforts to interpret biblical apocalyptic and eschatology as arbitrary exercises of divine power. As such, as Sir Isaac Newton and other moderns asserted, the final catastrophe would only be understood at final age of the world, so moderns often present themselves as at the final stage of the world.[6] Modern science rejected an approach to the universe in which attunement toward the whole of the world is needed by cultivating a metaphysical wisdom. Instead modern empirical science tended to concentrate upon individual things and events, seeking any relations among particular things as only an exercise of more or less arbitrary power. Where modern science would wrest knowledge as power from observing and instrumentalizing nature, so modern fundamentalists would wrest from biblical apocalyptic eschatology by various exegetical instruments the secrets of the end time as immanent.[7]

Aquinas's sapiential eschatology is most important to overcome these tendencies toward instrumentalizing both nature and divine revelation. He also overcomes the dualisms of soul and body, subjectivist mind and

---

4 *Summa contra Gentiles* II, 24, 4: "ordo enim aliquorum ad invicem est propter ordinem eorum ad finem."

5 See Brian Daley, SJ, *The Hope of the Early Church: A Handbook of Patristic Eschatology* (Cambridge: Cambridge University Press, 1991).

6 Sir Isaac Newton, *Observations Upon the Prophecies of Daniel and the Apocalypse of St. John* (1733).

7 Eschatology and apocalyptic as catastrophic destruction of the universe is commonplace in much contemporary scientific and popular writings, cf. J. V. Schall, SJ, "Apocalyptic as a Secular Enterprise," *Scottish Journal of Theology* 29 (1976): 357–73; Tim LaHaye, *Left Behind: A Novel of the Earth's Last Days* (Carol Stream IL: Tyndale, 2000); Paul Thigpen, *The Rapture Trap: A Catholic Response to "End Times" Fever* (New York: Ascension Press, 2001).

objectivist matter, that underpin instrumental rationality and so derail not a few modern efforts at understanding eschatology.[8] This dualism is rooted in the modern failure to appreciate, as Aquinas's sapiential eschatology does, how the revelation of eschatology in Holy Scripture supernaturally fulfills the finality of the created universe rather than simply destroying and negating it in a final conflagration. The trials of the end time are not the final act in the drama of human history but the birth pangs to the eternal consummation of the universe and history in the kingdom of God.[9]

Not surprisingly, therefore, the whole of Aquinas's theology is a knowledge subaltern to the knowledge of God and of the blessed.[10] The interplay of metaphysical wisdom and revealed wisdom is masterfully elaborated in his treatment of the divine essence and the distinction of the three divine persons. The Greek and Latin fathers had drawn upon the philosophical contemplative wisdom that clearly differentiated the intelligible from the sensible. St. Augustine dramatized this in the narrative of his own gradual intellectual conversion as he came to understand that God is infinite intelligence and love transcending all material and imaginable images. Indeed, he came to this realization by discovering how his own mind was spiritual.[11]

As Augustine had indicated how the intellectual and moral excellence advocated by the best of the philosophers could be lived only through his conversion to Jesus Christ, so Aquinas indicates how the intellectual and moral virtues are integrated within the absolutely supernatural communion with the Triune God operative in the theological virtues of faith, hope, and charity.[12]

Aquinas's treatment of the divine essence, divine knowledge, love, providence, and beatitude is a masterful theoretical exposition of the analogous knowledge of God that springs from the metaphysical wisdom of such an intellectual conversion. Only in this context of an explanatory exposi-

---

8 Cf. Rudolf Bultmann, *History and Eschatology* (New York: Harper & Row, 1962) on the problem of eschatology as a doctrine of the destruction of the world, only to turn eschatological passages into a subjectivist existential "now time" of the believer. See also Andre Malet, *La Pensee de Rudolf Bultmann: Mythos et Logos* (Geneva: Labor et Fides, 1962).

9 Contemporary scholarship is indicating how apocalyptic eschatology involves transformative symbols of the transcendent, see Daley, *The Hope of the Early Church*; Bernard McGuinn, *Visions of the End* (New York: Crossroad, 1979).

10 *ST* I, q. 1, a. 2.

11 St. Augustine, *Confessions*, especially books 5 through 9; see also chapter 3 above.

12 See *ST*, II–II, 23, 7 and 8.

tion of the Divine Being, Knowing, Loving, can Aquinas then develop the revealed interpersonal distinctions of Father, Son, and Holy Spirit as in the simplicity and unity of the divine nature.[13]

This synthesis of philosophical and theological wisdom set an immense task for Aquinas's eschatology. Without the light of faith, philosophers had tended to ascribe evil to matter and a resulting weakness in the human mind. The Averroists at the University of Paris made it imperative that Aquinas indicate how theological wisdom can overcome the limitations of an unenlightened metaphysics that turns the distinction of the intelligible and sensible into an opposition and contradiction.[14] As grace perfects nature, so the revelation of the last things perfects the finality of all of creation.

Everything created is made "for the divine goodness itself," for God "does not create in order to acquire some end" extrinsic to himself. In creating all things, "He intends only to communicate His own perfection, which is His goodness." This divine goodness means that each and every creature "intends to attain its own perfection, which is a likeness of divine perfection and goodness."[15] Indeed, it is precisely the wise ordering of all things to the infinitely transcendent divine goodness, that assures the ultimate unity of all created things in their multiple and dazzling diversities.[16]

As the divine act of creating is "the emanation of all being from the universal cause who is God,"[17] and the finality of all created things is the divine goodness, so a primary differentiation of things is in terms of good and evil, where evil cannot exist of itself but only as the privation or absence of good. The very diversity of things means that corruption, as a privation of good, can occur insofar as something either is not what it should be, or willfully acts in disordered, evil ways.[18] Only intelligent

---

[13] For an excellent study of Aquinas, and how he draws upon Augustine, cf. D. Juvenal Merriell, *To The Image of the Trinity: A Study in the Development of Aquinas' Teaching* (Toronto: Pontifical Institute of Medieval Studies, 1990).

[14] These difficulties can be seen in the condemnations of 219 propositions by the Bishop of Paris in 1277. The final seven regarded eschatology.

[15] *ST* I, q. 44, a. 4.

[16] *ST* I, q. 47, a. 3. Note that this is a theological statement: The unity of the created world is relative to the creator; it does not mean that there could not be many worlds or universes. In commenting on John 3:24, "For he gives the Spirit without measure," Aquinas makes the startling affirmation that the grace of Christ is not only more than sufficient to save the entire world, but that it is more than sufficient to save "even many worlds, if they were to exist": *Super Evangelium S. Ioannis Lectura,* 5th ed., ed. Raphaelis Cai, OP (Rome: Marietti, 1952), 3, lect. 6, no. 544.

[17] *ST* I, q. 45, a. 1.

[18] *ST* I, q. 45, aa. 1 and 4; q. 48, aa. 1–6.

creatures can act evilly, willfully turning away from the wisdom of the divine order. Yet even this evil of sin can never totally corrupt the good created by God, let alone frustrate his divine wisdom.[19]

So at the very beginning of his analysis of creation Aquinas introduces what stymied the best of the Greek and Latin philosophers: evil. The best of acquired human wisdom was unequal to the task of showing how all is ordered to divine wisdom and goodness. The creation of angels and humankind indicates how the drama of human history is caught up in the larger drama of angelic worship and demonic fall and hate.[20] This indicates how the problem of evil is not due to material creation, which is revealed as good, but to a spiritual pride that only intelligent creatures can cause by willfully turning away from the divinely ordered wisdom.

Wisdom attends to the whole of the creation as divinely ordered and redeemed, so Aquinas indicates how no amount of evil agents and actions can thwart God's wisdom. Citing Dionysius and Augustine, Aquinas provides a fundamental principle of sapiential eschatology, one that was reiterated by many Greek and Latin Fathers: Just as God alone can create out of nothing, so God alone can bring good out of evil:

> God and nature and any other agent make what is best in the whole, but not what is best in every single part, except in order to the whole, as was said above (47, 2). And the whole itself, which is the universe of creatures, is all the better and more perfect if some things in it can fail in goodness, and do sometimes fail, God not preventing this. This happens, firstly, because "it belongs to Providence not to destroy, but to save nature," as Dionysius says (*De Divinis Nominibus* iv); but it belongs to nature that what may fail should sometimes fail; secondly, because, as Augustine says (*Enchiridion* 11), "God is so powerful that He can even make good out of evil." Hence many good things would be taken away if God permitted no evil to exist; for fire would not be generated if air was not corrupted, nor would the life of a lion be preserved unless the ass were killed. Neither would avenging justice nor the patience of a sufferer be praised if there were no iniquity.[21]

---

[19] *ST* I, q. 48, a. 4. Aquinas says that even if sins were added infinitely, ever more lessening someone's ability *(habilitas)* to receive grace, still such an ability could never be totally taken away since it belongs to the nature of sinner that is created for the good.

[20] *ST* I, qq. 50–74.

[21] *ST* I, q. 48, a. 2, ad 3.

The justice of wisdom is central to Aquinas's eschatology. First of all there is the justice of our worship and praise to the all just and good God, whose infinite love brings good out of evil and so enables us to respond in faith, hope, and charity. If the theological virtues have God as their proper object, the moral virtue of religion, as integral to justice, fosters acts of devotion in the will, and acts of prayer in the reason. The "Our Father" indicates how all prayer is eschatologically oriented to the glory of God and the coming of his kingdom.[22] All the acts of religion, like prayer, devotion, adoration, worship, sacrifices, and vows render what is due to the Triune God as the end or final cause of all creation.[23]

The justice of divine wisdom is also manifested in the longing of hope for that eternal kingdom of God where the full redemption of human history will be manifest. "If we have hoped in Christ in this life only, we are of all men most to be pitied" (1 Cor 15:19). Commenting on this verse Aquinas indicates the importance of our eschatological hope for eternal life in the Risen Lord for their personal, intellectual, and moral excellence of the Apostles, Christians, and all human beings:

> If there is no resurrection from the dead, it follows that only in this life would humans have anything good; and if this is so, then those are the more miserable who in this life suffer many evils and tribulations. Since, therefore, the Apostles and Christians suffer many tribulations, it follows that they are more miserable than other men who at least enjoy the goods of this world. . . . Moreover, man naturally desires the welfare [*salutem*] of his very self. However, the soul is only a part of an embodied human being, and is not the whole human being, so the soul is not the self or "I." Thus if only the soul gained welfare in another life, it would not be the self or "I" or any unique human being. And besides, since man naturally desires the welfare of even his body, a natural desire would be frustrated. . . . Moreover, the good of the intellect is truth, and so if there were no resurrection their faith would have been false . . . and the good of morals requires the resurrection so that all that they gave up of the pleasures of this life and despising death itself not be reputed as utter foolishness.[24]

---

22 *ST* II–II, qq. 81–83; q. 83, a. 9.
23 *ST* II–II, q. 81, a. 5; qq. 84–91.
24 *Super Primam Epistolam ad Corinthios Lectura in Super Epistolas S. Pauli Lectura*, ed. Raphael Cai, OP, 8th revised ed. (Rome: Marietti, 1953), 923–25.

Without the future life the present life becomes futile and all work for truth, goodness, and justice collapses in futility. For both good and evil persons die, and no matter how justice is meted out in this life, no human justice can raise the dead and make whole the broken and murdered lives of so many victims of injustice and hate. That is why, in line with how grace perfects nature, Aquinas defines a general notion of justice as including "the proper ordination of man to God" and so in this sense includes the justification of sinful man, the theological virtues of faith, hope, and charity, with their fulfillment in eternal beatitude.[25]

No finite being can fulfill the desires of the human mind and heart. In accord with his emphasis upon wisdom, Aquinas indicates how ultimate and perfect human happiness or beatitude can only be realized in knowing and loving the Infinitely intelligent and loving cause of all that is, the Triune God.[26] Here the immaterial image of God in the human mind finds a fulfillment beyond anything we could humanly hope for in this world. Just as the context for humanly acquired virtues is friendship, so the theological virtues result from the forgiving and infinitely generous friendship of the Triune God, who wisely loved us into being, and even more wisely redeemed us from sin in the life, death, and resurrection of the Word Incarnate, Jesus Christ.[27] In this life we come to know God through the effects he causes. By charity, however, we love God immediately and directly, and love all else through God.[28] In heaven the blessed enjoy a cognitive immediacy proportionate to their immediacy with God in charity:

> . . . the more the intellect is participating in the light of glory the more perfectly will it see God. But it will participate more in the light of glory the more it has charity since where charity is greater there is greater desire; and desire somehow makes the one desiring more apt and ready to receive what is desired. Hence the more anyone will have of charity, the more perfectly will he see God and the more blessed will he be.[29]

25 *De veritate* 28, 1; 4, ad 11; *De perfectione spiritualis vitae* 13: "For as human beings are consorts of one city, all under one prince and governed by his laws, so also all men, inasmuch as they naturally tend toward beatitude, have a certain general congruity in their order to God as to the highest principle of all and font of beatitude and the legislator of the whole of justice."

26 *ST* I–II, qq. 3, 8.

27 *ST* II–II, q. 23; q. 26, a. 13; q. 27, a. 3, ad 2.

28 *ST* II–II, q. 27, a. 4.

29 *ST* I, q. 12, a. 6.

It is important to recall the "order of wisdom"—it is not that the infused habit of charity or the light of glory mediates the immediacy of the Triune God to us. Rather it is the immediacy of God's interpersonal presence that causes the created effects of the habit of charity and the light of glory. United in ecstatic intimacy with the Triune God, the blessed know the Triune God and simultaneously know all other things in the Divine Word. The intimacy of communion with God in the beatific vision is analogous to the intimate union of soul and body, for God himself will be united immediately to the beatified created intelligence.[30]

To grasp both the intimacy and ecstasy of the blessed communion with the Trinity, reflect on all the great insights and discoveries and knowledge of your entire life, and of the whole of human history—all the great discoveries and knowledge. That would be but a flicker of the understanding and knowledge enjoyed by the blessed in heaven. Think of all the acts of love you have experienced in your entire life, and join to those all the acts of love of each and every human being through the whole course of history. All of that love would be no more than a spark compared to the infinite love of the Triune God. Each and every blessed is enraptured in infinite understanding, generating infinite knowledge, spirating infinite love. Our human minds and hearts are indeed restless until they rest in this divine beatitude.

The blessed know the divine wisdom that redeems us through the Word Incarnate, and why this wisdom chose not to remove evil through power, but to transform evil into good through the mysterious life, death, and resurrection of Jesus Christ. This beatific wisdom will completely fulfill the most profound desires of our minds and hearts. The specific desire of human nature is to know truth and love the good. We desire to understand everything, knowing both individual things and all things. There is no opposition between the universal and the particular, the individual person and the

---

[30] *ST* I, q. 12, aa. 9 and 10; Suppl., 92, 1: "As from the natural form (whereby a thing has being) and matter, there results one thing simply, so from the form whereby the intellect understands, and the intellect itself, there results one thing intelligibly. . . . Hence if there be a self-subsistent reality, that has nothing in itself besides that which is intelligible, such a reality can by itself be the form whereby the intellect understands. Now a thing is intelligible in respect of its actuality and not of its potentiality (*Met.* ix): in proof of which an intelligible form needs to be abstracted from matter and from all the properties of matter. Therefore, since the Divine essence is pure act, it will be possible for it to be the form whereby the intellect understands: and this will be the beatific vision. Hence the Master says (*Sent.* ii, d. 50, c. 6) that the union of the body with the soul is an illustration of the blissful union of the spirit with God." From this it does not follow that the blessed become divine, cf. ibid., ad 9.

human race. The light of reason is elevated and healed by the light of charity-informed faith, this in turn is elevated by the light of glory. All are ever higher created participations in the Divine Eternal Light who is the Triune God.[31]

One of the great joys of the beatific vision will be finally to understand the beauty and wisdom of each and every thing that has occurred in our own lives, in the lives of those we love, and indeed in the whole of human history. The blessed will understand why God allowed the evil and sin to murder and scare so many, and how God's wisdom and Christ's redemptive mission has transformed all of that evil and suffering into goodness and glory. This understanding will be such that even the most insignificant event will be finally intelligible within the beauty of the whole of creation. Why this daughter died in infancy, why such a promising son was cut down by an auto accident, why that father was murdered, why that mother was so brutally raped. All of these most painful questions and "whys" that spring from what to our feeble minds and hearts are countless histories of suffering, all will be answered in the joy of the beatific vision. As the risen Christ's glorified body had the wounds of his passion, so the blessed will understand how God's wisdom transformed both their own sins and sufferings as well as those of all others, including the justice of any damned in hell.[32] The special gifts and auras of each of the blessed will show forth the harmony and beauty of the whole of creation in the symphonic glory of the entire created universe.[33]

The Resurrection of the Whole Body of Christ

This leads us to the bodily resurrection. During his earthly life Jesus Christ in his human knowledge knew by the light of glory what faithful Christians believe because of his teachings.[34] The more we love someone, the more we suffer in his or her sufferings. The more we love someone, the more our hearts are broken when they offend us. Divine wisdom chose to redeem us, not by removing evil through power, but by transforming evil into good through suffering. So the Word became incarnate. He whose infinite love creates all things, loving them into existence, becomes man to redeem sinful humans through his passion and death.

---

31 *De veritate* 18, 1, ad 1; *ST* I, q. 84, a. 5; *In Boethius de Trinitate,* 1, 3, ad 1.

32 *ST* Suppl., qq. 93, 94.

33 *ST* Suppl, qq. 95, 96.

34 *ST* III, q. 9, a. 2. See Guy Mansini, O.S.B., "Understanding St. Thomas on Christ's Immediate Knowledge of Christ," *The Thomist* 59 (1995): 91–124.

The fact that Jesus Christ in his human consciousness had not the light of faith, as we do, but the light of glory, in no way dulled his pain, suffering, and sorrow. Since he was not yet glorified in his humanity, the light of glory did the opposite. The higher the created consciousness, the greater will be the suffering. As a weak analogy might put it, someone with a finely tuned ear for music will suffer more intensely when someone sings off key. Knowing and loving the Triune God both divinely and humanly, only Christ's human nature united hypostatically to the Word could take up into his human mind and heart each and every human being with all his and her sins and sufferings. Jesus Christ as the divine Person of the Word Incarnate suffered more than all the sufferings of human beings throughout history put together.

Indeed, he gathered into his heart each and every human being in all the uniqueness of each and every one of us. Every human being is present in Christ's human mind and heart, as the beloved is present in the lover, the known present in the knower. The concrete universality of all the uniquely individual and most painful histories of suffering are present in Christ's love for each and every one of us on the Cross.[35] So it is that we are baptized into Christ's death. And so it is that we fill up in our own lives what is wanting in the sufferings of Christ, for as disciples of Christ the Church carries forward the visible mission of the Word Incarnate in her sacramental rendering present Christ in his paschal mystery.[36]

So the sapiential eschatology of Aquinas situates the bodily resurrection within the context of the paschal mystery. In the *Summa contra Gentiles* Aquinas introduces the resurrection of the body after discussing the sacrament of marriage as embodying the love of Christ for his Church.[37] Since the first man brought sin into the world, and through sin death (Romans 5:12), so Christ redeems us from both sin and, at the end of the world, death. The resurrection of the body is caused by the resurrection of Christ.[38] Aquinas indicates how faith in the resurrection of the body in no way contradicts what we know of human nature by reason. Reading his

---

[35] *ST* III, q. 10, a. 2; q. 46, aa. 5–8. Note the importance of the highest Christology possible, as it is defined by the great Councils, if one is going to take the concrete histories of suffering seriously. Only God incarnate can redeem a human history, each page of which is stained with so much suffering and blood.

[36] *ST* III, q. 66, a. 2.

[37] *SCG* IV, 78–79.

[38] *ST* Suppl., q. 76, a. 1.

reflections over seven centuries later, it is remarkable how the metaphysical principles validly illuminate the issues involved.[39]

A wisdom approach emphasizes the *intelligibility* of the cosmos and of all that God creates and redeems. Any miraculous character of events does not mean their "unintelligibility" as if God were doing something irrational. Rather, there are events that we cannot understand by the light of reason, but their intelligibility will be understood by the light of glory. What we know by faith as miraculous we shall understand by the light of glory. Hence the efforts of the Fathers and Aquinas to offer natural analogues to provide a fruitful but imperfect understanding, at least insofar as what is affirmed in faith does not contradict the truths of reason. They take up a series of possible objections to the resurrection of the body, responding to them.[40]

Aquinas's metaphysics demands the kind of intellectual conversion recounted by Augustine in order to understand how the intelligibility of the human soul causes the corporality of the human person. Thus he is able to dispatch the concerns of those who point to the obliteration, disintegration, or disappearance of corpses. As he writes:

> None of any human's essential principles yields entirely to nothingness in death, for the rational soul which is man's form remains after death, . . . the matter, also, which was subject to such a form remains in the same dimensions which made it able to be the individual matter. Therefore, by conjunction to a soul numerically the same a human being will be restored to matter numerically the same.[41]

Due to nominalism and a pervasive Cartesian dualism, contemporaries tend to imagine that body and soul are two different things, much as Descartes's *res cogitans* and *res extensa*. Various forms of idealism cling to the former, while forms of empiricism cling to the latter for their definitions of reality. Soul and body are not, for Aquinas, two distinct things but components of one reality, a human being. Thus he can write that an immortal soul without bodily resurrection would satisfy neither the promises of the Gospel nor

---

39 See, for example, Bernard Lonergan, SJ, *Insight: A Study of Human Understanding* (Toronto: University of Toronto Press, 1992), 410–617; Benedict Ashley, OP, *Theologies of the Body: Humanist and Christian* (Braintree, MA: Pope John Center, 1995), 565–645; John Wippel, *The Metaphysical Thought of Thomas Aquinas: From Finite Being to Uncreated Being* (Washington, DC: Catholic University of America Press, 2000).

40 St. Augustine, *De Civitate Dei* XXII; *ST* Suppl., qq. 75–86; *SCG* IV, 81–90.

41 *SCG* IV, 81, 7.

the deepest desires of the human heart. For, Aquinas argues, human beings cannot attain perfect happiness, beatitude, and justice in this life, therefore the resurrection is needed if human beings are to realize their natural and supernatural end willed by God.[42]

Throughout his resolution of objections to bodily resurrection, Aquinas maintains the God-given dignity of individual persons. God's knowledge and love creates the totality of all things and the singularity and uniqueness of each and every thing.[43] The resurrection guarantees the unique singularity of each and every human being, with the fullness of their individual personhood, will be rewarded or punished according to their own unique responses to God's loving gifts to them. Thus Aquinas shows that human beatitude requires specifically human and personally individual resurrection, not some vague or abstract perpetuation of the species:

> Wherefore *humanity* signifies nothing else besides the essential principles of the species; so that its signification is only partial. On the other hand *man* signifies the essential principles of the species, without excluding the principles of individuality from its signification: since man signifies one having humanity, and this does not exclude his having other things: wherefore its signification is complete, because it signifies the essential principles of the species actually, and the individualizing principles potentially. But *Socrates* signifies both actually, even as the genus includes the difference potentially, whereas the species includes it actually. From this it follows that both the very same man and the very same humanity rise again, by reason of the survival of the rational soul, and the unity of matter.[44]

He goes on to point out how the mystery of the resurrection, while natural insofar as "it is natural for the soul to be united to the body," is not natural in its cause since that is the divine power alone that can bring it about.[45]

We know that there are billions upon billions of human beings who have, are, and will live and die. Each and every one of them has an immortal soul, which, Aquinas points out, is the substantial form of each and every human being. There is a unique individuality to each and every human being. Aquinas sees the resurrection of the body as the clear testimony to the profound interpersonal character of all the Triune God does for us. As he

---

42 *ST* Suppl., q. 75, aa. 1–3.
43 *ST* I, q. 14, a. 11.
44 *SCG* IV, 81, 10.
45 *SCG* IV, 81, 14.

remarks, if God only intended the immortality of the human race as a species, generation would suffice for that.

> But the resurrection is not ordered to the perpetuity of the species, for this could be safeguarded by generation. It must then be ordered to the perpetuity of the individual: but not to the soul alone, for the soul already had perpetuity before the resurrection. Therefore it regards the perpetuity of the composite. Man rising, therefore, will live forever.[46]

The interpersonal intimacy is such that the risen glorified bodies are totally transformed to be fully iconic of the holiness and love of the Triune God and the Risen Jesus. Intussusceptive and reproductive functions are no longer present in the immortal and transformed human persons in the ecstacy of ever fuller understanding and love of the Triune God. That there is no food or sex in heaven is a tribute to the iconic beauty of each and every embodied human person. The bodies of the blessed will be totally transparent in the joy and ecstacy of communion in the Body of Christ.[47]

Aquinas's sapiential eschatology attends to the whole in a way that far from neglecting individuals realizes how God knows and loves each and every human being into being. Only an Infinitely Wise and Loving Father could know and love through the Holy Spirit so many countless human persons into existence as members of the mystical body of his own Son, the Word Incarnate. They are not "countless" or an "abstraction" to God's Infinite Intelligence and Love, each and every one is known and loved as only God knows and loves them.[48] The ultimate dignity of the human person is his or her eschatological communion with all the blessed in the new heavens and new earth of the eternal Kingdom of God:

> Accordingly, just as the soul that enjoys the vision of God will be filled with spiritual brightness, so by a kind of overflow from the soul to the body, the latter will be, in its own way, clothed with the brightness of glory. Hence the Apostle says (1 Cor 15:18): "It is sown," namely the body, "in dishonor, it shall rise in glory": because now this body of ours is opaque, whereas then it will be translucent, according to Matthew 13:43: "Then shall the just shine like the sun in the kingdom of their Father."[49]

---

46 *SCG* IV, 82, 6.
47 *SCG* IV, 83–85.
48 *ST* I, q. 20, a. 2.
49 *SCG* IV, 86, 2.

Christ's Judgment: Reward and Punishment in the New Heavens and New Earth

Having already discussed the justice of divine wisdom in connection with creation, evil, and redemption in the first part of his *Summa theologiae*, it is important to realize how for Aquinas this is both profoundly personal and universal in Christ Jesus. Jesus Christ knows and loves each and every human being far better than any of us know ourselves. This concrete universality of Jesus Christ's knowledge and love of us is the theological reality of his judgment of each of us at our death, and all of us in the last judgment:

> When it is asked whether Christ knows all things in the Word, "all things" may be taken . . . properly to mean that "all things" include whatsoever is, will be, or was done, said, or thought, by whomsoever and at any time. And in this way it must be said that the soul of Christ knows all things in the Word. . . . Now everything belongs to Christ and to His dignity, inasmuch as "all things are subject to Him" (I Cor. 15:27). Moreover, He has been appointed Judge of all by God, "because He is the Son of Man," as is stated in John 5:27; and therefore the soul of Christ knows in the Word all things existing in whatever time, and the thoughts of men, of which He is the Judge, so that what is said of Him (John 2:25), "For He knew what was in man," can be understood not merely of the Divine knowledge, but also of His soul's knowledge, which it had in the Word.[50]

The judgment of Christ manifests both the justice and mercy of God insofar as he who judges us is the one who suffered for us on the cross.[51]

---

[50] *ST* III, q. 10, a. 2.

[51] *ST* III, q. 14, a. 2; q. 59, aa. 2 and 3; Suppl. q. 90, a. 1; *Super ad Hebraeos* 2, 4. Both justice and mercy are present in Christ's freeing mankind of sin, cf. *ST* III, q. 46, a. 1, ad 3: "That man should be delivered by Christ's Passion was in keeping with both His mercy and His justice. With His justice, because by His Passion Christ made satisfaction for the sin of the human race; and so man was set free by Christ's justice: and with His mercy, for since man of himself could not satisfy for the sin of all human nature, as was said above (1, 2), God gave him His Son to satisfy for him, according to Rm 3:24,25: 'Being justified freely by His grace, through the redemption that is in Christ Jesus, whom God hath proposed to be a propitiation, through faith in His blood.' And this came of more copious mercy than if He had forgiven sins without satisfaction. Hence it is said (Eph. 2:4): 'God, who is rich in mercy, for His exceeding charity wherewith He loved us, even when we were dead in sins, hath quickened us together in Christ.' "

Wisdom attends to the whole of the creation as divinely ordered and redeemed, so Aquinas indicates that the judgment of Christ reveals that no amount of evil agents and actions can thwart God's wisdom. Those intellectual agents who willfully turn a created good away from the divinely ordered wisdom—which is always a violent removal of the particular good from its order—suffer the just punishments due such acts. The evil of such punishments are indeed willed by God's all good wisdom, where the evil of sin is not so willed by God. For in sinning any agent is violently offending his own being and nature. Again, it is only in the perspective of Aquinas's sapiential eschatology that we can understand the mystery of divine justice and mercy. It is only in the context of nominalism and voluntarism that predestination and damnation were misunderstood as exercises of an inscrutable divine power. In the wisdom perspective that places the intelligibility of all of reality as present in the Divine Infinite Intelligence and Love of God, one can appreciate how it is precisely because of the Divine Intelligence, Love, Justice, and Mercy that God respects the free decisions of intelligent creatures. Aquinas's analysis of the punishments of the damned indicates how God respects the choices they have made in turning away from the Divine Goodness. They violently frustrated the natural orientation of their minds and wills toward the good, and therefore seek to disrupt the goodness of the created order.[52]

What is central in a sapiential eschatology is precisely the intelligence and reason operative in the divine wisdom. Could intelligent creatures frustrate the order of creation by their prideful self-assertion to disrupt that order through violently removing some particular good from its orientation toward God? If so, then a consequence would be the possibility of a radical depersonalization of the universe by evil. The Triune God would not be God! Thus it is for the good of the wise order of the whole universe that evil angels and humans suffer the punishments of hell:

> It must be granted that God inflicts punishments, not for his own sake, as though he took pleasure in them, but for the sake of something else: namely on account of the order that must be imposed on creatures, in which order the good of the universe consists. Now, the order of things demands that all things be dispensed by God proportionally; for which reason it is said (Wisdom 11:21) that God does all things in *weight, number and measure*. And, as rewards correspond proportionally to acts

---

52 *ST* Suppl., q. 98, aa. 1–5.

of virtue, so do punishments to sins: and to some sins eternal punishment is proportionate, as we have proved. Therefore for certain sins God inflicts eternal punishment that in things there may be maintained the right order which shows forth His wisdom.[53]

This wisdom of divine justice is well illustrated in Dante's *Divine Comedy* where those in hell and in purgatory never complain that they should not be suffering the punishments they are; indeed, their state of punishment is precisely what their own evil actions have brought about.[54] They are the causes of their own damnation by their rejection of the orientation of their own beings toward the goodness of God. So Aquinas concludes that it would be unreasonable to expect that they could ever enjoy the beatific vision given the obstinacy of their opposition to the Divine goodness.[55] So also, their resurrected bodies do not share in the translucent beauty of ordered goodness, but rather in the dark suffering of their opposition to the light and beauty of the Triune God shining through the transformed new heavens and new earth.[56]

The sapiential eschatology of Aquinas, building upon patristic eschatologies, understands the eschatological and apocalyptic passages in Scripture as revealing the transformation of the whole of creation so that it fully manifests the divine wisdom, beauty, and goodness. This contrasts with those who view these passages as involving or portending widespread devastation or ultimate doom.[57] A wisdom approach indicates clearly how what is catastrophic from the viewpoint of this world is only the purification needed for transition to the Kingdom of God.[58] Because the whole material universe is created for human beings to give glory to God, so it will share in their glorious beatitude. Where sin and evil turns the universe into idolatrous darkness and disorder, grace and glory will render the universe fully iconic of the divine wisdom.

---

[53] *SCG* III, 144, 10.

[54] *ST* I, q. 47, a. 3; q. 48, aa. 3, 5, and 6; q. 49, a. 2. Cf. Robert Royal, *Dante Alighieri: Divine Comedy, Divine Spirituality* (New York: Crossroad, 1999); Anthony Cassell, *Dante's Fearful Art of Justice* (Toronto: University of Toronto Press, 1984).

[55] *ST* Suppl., q. 99, a. 3; *SCG* IV, 93–94.

[56] *ST* Suppl., q. 86; *SCG* IV, 89–90.

[57] Thus the various dictionary definitions of apocalyptic as "involving widespread devastation or ultimate doom," see also references in note 6 above.

[58] *SCG* IV, 97, 4–6.

In enjoying beatific communion with the Father in the Son with the Holy Spirit, the blessed will see how God has disposed all things with divine wisdom, how he brought good out of all the evil and suffering endured by all the blessed when they lived on earth. The final state of the whole of creation will find its glorious consummation in the ecstatic union of all the blessed with the Triune God: They will understand how their lives here on earth were conformed to the wisdom of Christ Jesus who redeemed us, not by removing evil through power, but by transforming evil into good through his passion, death, and resurrection. The whole cosmos will be transfigured in the glorious presence of the whole Christ in whom each and every one of the blessed will be enraptured in communion with each other in the infinite understanding and love of the Triune God.

> Since then the corporeal creation is disposed of finally in a manner that is in keeping with man's state, and since men themselves will not only be delivered from corruption, but also clothed in glory, as we have stated, it follows that even the material creation will acquire a certain glory of brightness befitting its capacity. Wherefore it is said in Revelations 21:1: *I saw a new heaven and a new earth:* and in Isaiah (65:17–18): *I create new heavens, and a new earth, and the former things shall not be in remembrance, and they shall not come upon the heart. But you shall be glad and rejoice for ever.* AMEN.[59]

---

[59] *SCG* IV, 97, 7–8; on how this is prefigured in the transfiguration of Christ, cf. *Lectura super Matthaeum*, caput 17, lect. 1.

Modernism and Americanism Revisited Dialectically: A Challenge for Evangelization

AFTER TWO MILLENNIA we are still only at the beginning of the mission of Christ to redeem the human race.

The mission of Christ the redeemer, which is entrusted to the church, is still very far from completion. As the second millennium after Christ's coming draws to an end, an overall view of the human race shows that this mission is still only beginning and that we must commit ourselves wholeheartedly to its service. [T]he church's function in every age, and particularly in ours, is to direct man's gaze, to point the awareness and experience of the whole of humanity toward the mystery of Christ.[1]

This is a wonderfully Catholic perspective on the call to evangelization that Pope John Paul II has issued from the beginning of his pontificate. The mission of the Church is the continuation down through all ages of the mission of the Word Incarnate. Especially in modern times it is important to acknowledge how what is new—in this case the "new evangelization"—does not contradict or oppose what was old.

Innovation does not negate tradition. There is a tension between tradition and innovation, and that tension is present in every age. It came to

---

This essay was originally published as "Modernism and Americanism Revisited Dialectically: A Challenge for Evangelization" in *Communio: International Catholic Review* XXXI (4; Winter 1994): 631–32.
[1] John Paul II, *Redemptoris Missio* §1.

the fore in the Second Vatican Council, as its two tasks were usually seen as both a *ressourcement*, a recovery of the tradition, and an *aggiornomento*, a bringing up-to-date, an innovation. It has ever been the responsibility of the teaching authority of the Church and theologians to foster both elements, without letting one overrule or negate the other.

In this essay I shall first revisit Catholicism's criticisms of modernism and Americanism. This revisiting will be dialectical rather than historical. Theologians have unfinished work in these areas. I indicate how the new dedication to evangelization called for by John Paul II points the way toward transforming modern cultures. Then I shall outline some major dialectical differences between Catholicism and philosophical and theological implications of modernism and Americanism. These dialectical differences, it seems to me, are among the most important intellectual tasks facing the evangelization of modern cultures, and I shall briefly mention the Catholic resources for responding to these tasks.

Modernism and Americanism Revisited

There are many disputes about the history and prehistory of modernity, about the relative importance of Machiavelli or Hobbes, of the Renaissance humanists or Descartes, of nominalism and the European wars of religion.[2] No serious scholar, however, disputes that a central tenet of modernism was to emphasize the differences between the old and the new, between the ancients and the moderns.

From History to Dialectics

I do not propose to revisit the many histories of modernism and Americanism. The historical investigations are ongoing and too extensive to permit any easy overview or summary.[3] In any event, all historians and theologians

[2] Cf. Leo Strauss, "The Three Waves of Modernity," in his *An Introduction to Political Philosophy*, ed. H. Gildin (Detroit: Wayne State University Press, 1989); Louis Dupré, *Passage to Modernity* (New Haven, CT: Yale University Press, 1993); Stanley Rosen, *The Ancients and the Moderns: Rethinking Modernity* (New Haven, CT: Yale University Press, 1989); Hans Blumenberg, *The Legitimacy of the Modern Age* (Cambridge, MA: MIT Press, 1983); Luc Ferry, *Rights: The New Quarrel between the Ancients and the Moderns* (Chicago: University of Chicago Press, 1990); J. Habermas, *The Philosophical Discourse of Modernity: Twelve Lectures*, trans. Fred Lawrence (Cambridge: MIT Press, 1987).

[3] Cf. Thomas Michael Loome, *Liberal Catholicism, Reform Catholicism, Modernism* (Mainz: Grünewald, 1977); also the works cited in notes 34–38, 43, and 46 below; also a recent issue of *U.S. Catholic Historian* 11 (Summer 1993) on Americanism.

are prepared to admit that there are *differences* between Catholicism, on the one hand, and both modernism and Americanism, on the other hand. Some will say that those differences are now lessened because of accommodation, usually on the part of Catholicism.

Generally, there are three types of differences: complementary, genetic, or dialectical.[4] Complementary differences promote a larger whole by each fulfilling different roles, tasks, histories—they support and complement each other: for example, the differences of man and woman, wife and husband, lawyer and doctor.[5] Differences can be genetic as in differences in stages of development: the differences between the seed and the grown plant, the fetus and the child, the child and the adult, an earlier and a later stage of a historical institution or movement. Finally, differences are dialectical when they present contradictory positions, such as good and evil, virtue and vice, grace and sin, truth and falsehood.

As historians continue to study modernism and Americanism there is going to emerge a clarification of the differences between Catholicism and modernism or Americanism as not only complementary and/or genetic, but also as those that remain to this day dialectical differences. There are some evaluations of both modernism and Americanism that, in my judgment, fail to attend to the dialectical differences. Some historians and theologians are of the opinion that Vatican II effectively silenced any serious concern for a dialectics of Americanism and modernism—as if the council had finally decided that the differences were only complementary and/or genetic. But such an evaluation overlooks the rather obvious facts that, when it comes to Americanism and modernism, what the popes warned against are errors and tendencies that were very much a part of the modern cultural horizons in Europe and America.

It is not difficult to summarize the dialectical contradictions. In *Testem Benevolentiae* (1899), Leo XIII warned about an Americanism that tended to "ignore catholic wisdom" and, in its eagerness to win converts to Catholicism, could compromise Catholic doctrines and practices, improperly accommodating them to the spirit of the age. Americanism dispenses with external or historically visible mediations of the Church; the Spirit

---

[4] Cf. Bernard Lonergan, SJ, *Method in Theology* (New York: Herder & Herder, 1972), 236–37; also his *Insight: A Study of Human Understanding* (Toronto: University of Toronto Press, 1992), 242–67, 426–55, 484–507.

[5] Cf. Pope John Paul II, *Christifideles Laici* §50 on the "diversity yet mutual complementarity" of the personhood of men and women, as well as the respective roles and functions they have.

alone suffices for individual guidance. The natural virtues were given priority over the supernatural virtues, the active virtues over the passive. Religious life dedicated to living the vows was played down in favor of associations without vows.[6]

These pastoral concerns were later linked with a modernism Pius X condemned in *Pascendi* (1907) as rooted in an *agnosticism* that denied the ability of the human mind to know that God exists, thereby limiting human reason to only an *immanentism* without divine transcendence. Faith is then *privatized (in privata cuiusque hominis experientia),* cut off from public knowledge and science, as if faith was not a knowledge of the realities revealed in faith. Thus Catholic dogmas are reduced to *mere symbols* or *myths,* rather than as stating the true realities revealed by God. Historical criticism is seen as destroying the sacred realities revealed in Scripture and doctrine. Faith only deals with ideas, symbols, myths.[7]

These elements against which the popes warned are clearly contradictory to Catholic faith and practice. The differences are, therefore, dialectical rather than complementary or genetic. As with any dialectic in Catholic theology, it is important to emphasize from the start that these contradictions are not the whole story. There are many very positive aspects in modern cultures and in American culture. Indeed, those positive dimensions can only be fostered insofar as the negative errors are corrected.

While historians are concerned with all the variations and complexities of a particular person's work, or of an epoch or of a movement, dialectics brings out the contradictory elements within a person's work, or in an epoch or movement. Historians are concerned with providing a narrative that will capture all the colors and textures of their subject matter, as if they were painting a portrait. Dialectics, however, is more like an X-ray highlighting contrasts that lie below the surface, revealing tendencies of which the persons involved often had either no knowledge or, if they did, may not have intended. We carry around colored photographs of our loved ones, but X-rays are vitally important when it is a question of their health. It is so also with *sana doctrina* or healthy teachings. When the ecclesial magisterium condemns and/or warns against certain errors or tendencies, it is engaging in dialectical discernment.

---

6 Cf. H. Denzinger and A. Schönmetzer, eds., *Enchiridion Symbolorum* (Freiburg: Herder, 1963), §3340–46; Thomas Wangler, "Americanist Beliefs and Papal Orthodoxy: 1884–1899" in *U.S. Catholic Historian* 11 (3; Summer 1993): 37–54.

7 Cf. *Enchiridion Symbolorum* §3475–3500, especially 3484.

For investigators the exercise of dialectics setting out positions and counterpositions will appear rather foggy to the extent that the investigator has not deepened an appropriation of the intellectual, moral, and religious realities toward which the dialectic moves. Indeed, a historical investigation might indicate that particular "modernists" or "Americanists" might have intended quite the opposite than the counterpositions of the movements condemned. But in history intentions are hardly indicative of the actual course of historical movements. The plans of a general, indicating his intentions, do not reveal the actual course of the battle. The delicate process of transforming or converting secularist and sensate cultures requires immense intellectual, moral, and religious differentiation.[8]

An Enlightenment Rejection of Catholicism

Enlightenment thinkers were quite explicit in their rejections of the ancient wisdom in favor of their new natural, human, social, and historical theories. There were no Enlightenment thinkers who praised the wisdom to be found in Roman Catholic faith and practice: quite the contrary. As Peter Gay put it so well, it was the emergence of modern paganism.[9] Charles Taylor rather acutely analyzes how the modern Enlightenment evaluation

---

8 Cf. Lonergan, *Method in Theology,* 235–93, 327ff. "On Americanism," cf. William Portier's "Inculturation as Transformation: The Case of Americanism Revisited," in *U.S. Catholic Historian* 11 (1993): 107–24. Also Newman wrote of the infallibility of Catholic teaching in a dialectical context, cf. John Henry Cardinal Newman, *Apologia Pro Vita Sua* (London: Collins Fontana Books, 1965), Part VII, 286: "The energy of the human intellect 'does from opposition grow;' it thrives and is joyous, with a tough elastic strength, under the terrible blows of the divinely-fashioned weapon, and is never so much itself as when it has lately been overthrown. . . . It is necessary for the very life of religion, viewed in its large operations and its history, that the warfare [between Authority and Private Judgment] should be incessantly carried on. Every exercise of Infallibility is brought out into act by an intense and varied operation of the Reason, from within and without, and provokes again a reaction of Reason against it; . . . [Catholicism] presents a continuous picture of Authority and Private Judgment alternately advancing and retreating as the ebb and flow of the tide;—it is a vast assemblage of human beings with willful intellects and wild passions, brought together into one by the beauty and majesty of a Superhuman Power—into what may be called a large reformatory or training-school, not to be sent to bed, not to be buried alive, but for the melting, refining, and molding, as in some moral factory, by an incessant noisy process . . . of the raw material of human nature, so excellent, so dangerous, so capable of divine purposes."

9 Peter Gay, *The Enlightenment: The Rise of Modern Paganism* (New York: Vintage, 1968).

of everyday life developed from the Protestant rejection of the Roman Catholic notion of an ecclesial and hierarchical mediation of the sacred.[10] In modern cultures there is no notion of the church in the full Catholic sense of sacramentally carrying forward the missions of the Son and Spirit. Each Christian is alone before God and is alone responsible for his or her personal commitment to Christ. If individual Catholics are passengers "in the ecclesial ship on its journey to God," for Protestants "there can be no passengers. This is because there is no ship in the Catholic sense, no common movement carrying humans to salvation. Each believer rows his or her own boat."[11] The bark of Peter was rather roundly denounced by Herder and Voltaire, Hobbes, Hume, and Locke. The Enlightenment and modernity were inimical to Catholic faith and practice.

Little wonder, then, that it was the dialectical differences, the contradictions, between Catholicism and modernity that stood out. In many respects modernism among Catholics can often have the effect of making Catholicism conform to the modern world, rather than an effort to transform the modern world in the light of Catholic faith. Yet the rhetoric of contradiction often failed to differentiate genuine contradictions from those elements in modernity that could be positively assimilated into Catholic tradition. Converting modern cultures to Christ, while a formidable task, required a careful discernment of what is good and what evil in modern cultures. The European wars of religion, as well as the contestations over the papal states, were dismantling the remnants of medieval Christendom. The challenge was to find in the modern period an analogue to the differentiation of sacerdotium and regnum of Christendom, and to manifest to modern cultures that being, truth, and goodness were not consequences of dominative power, but spring from divine wisdom, calling forth the importance of a Catholic *studium*, of a Catholic intellectual life that would meet the challenges of tradition and innovation.

The Catholic Effort at Differentiation

This double challenge was addressed pastorally in Vatican I and Vatican II. The declarations of Vatican I clearly differentiated the truth of God's revelation from typically modern conceptions of religious subjectivism, rationalism, and egalitarian reductionism, as if the truth of Christianity was no

---

10 Charles Taylor, *The Sources of the Self: The Making of Modern Identity* (Cambridge: Harvard University Press, 1989), 215ff.

11 Ibid., 217.

more than the consensus of a majority. The spiritual authority of the papacy was firmly defined and differentiated from its disappearing control over the papal states.

As with any process of dialectical differentiation, the separating out of the wheat and the chaff in modernity, there would be those who would fail to discern the differentiation and so reject it as either a betrayal of the tradition or a failure adequately to innovate. It was the latter that occurred after Vatican I as modernism. The dialectical meaning of modernism in Pascendi was articulated by Cardinal Mercier in a way that also raised an ambiguity that awaited clarification at Vatican II:

> Modernism is not the modern expression of science. . . . Modernism consists essentially in affirming that the religious soul must draw from itself, from nothing but itself, the object and motive of its faith. It rejects all revelation imposed upon the conscience, and thus, as a necessary consequence, becomes the negation of the doctrinal authority of the Church established by Jesus Christ, and it denies, moreover, to the divinely constituted hierarchy the right to govern Christian society.[12]

There was no way that Vatican II was ever reconciled to this modernism. It too rejected this subjectivism and reaffirmed the doctrinal authority of the Church. The final phrase in this quotation, however, shows an undifferentiated affirmation of a right to govern. What is meant by "Christian society?" It seems to be what John Courtney Murray described as the undifferentiated casting of a mantle of sacrality over a secular, socio-juridical order:

> The sacral conception had been the heritage of medieval Christendom and, in a far more ambiguous form, of the ancien régime. For our purposes here, two of its characteristics should be briefly noted. First, the Christian world—or at least the Catholic nation—was considered to be somehow enclosed within the Church, which was herself the one Great Society. Second, the religious prerogative of the prince extended to a care of the religion of his subjects and a care of their religious unity as essential to their political unity.[13]

---

[12] Cardinal Mercier, *Modernism,* trans. M. Lindsay (St. Louis, MO: Herder, 1910), 23.
[13] John Courtney Murray, SJ, "The Declaration on Religious Freedom," *Concilium* 15 (New York: Paulist Press, 1966), 6.

The extent to which "Christian society" would be understood within the context of an Ultramontane effort and ecclesiology, it is clear that Vatican II removed undifferentiated sacrality by differentiating sacred and secular, without dichotomizing them, and developing a *communio* ecclesiology that places the truth of Catholic faith in wisdom rather than power.[14]

Differentiation of Sacred and Secular in a Communio Ecclesiology

This *communio* ecclesiology clearly differentiates, without separating or juxtaposing one against the other, the political and the ecclesial. As *Gaudium et Spes* teaches:

> By virtue of its commission and competence the church is not identified in any way with political society or bound to any political system, being both a sign and a safeguard of the transcendence of the human person. The political community and the Church are independent of each other and autonomous in their respective spheres of activity. They are both at the service of the personal and social vocation of the same individuals, but under different titles.[15]

Karol Cardinal Wojtyla wrote in *Sources of Renewal*:

> Analyzing the problem of a just relationship between the political community and the Church, it [the Council] emphasizes that a clear distinction should be made "between the activities of Christians acting individually or collectively in their own name, as citizens guided by the dictates of a Christian conscience, and their activity acting along with their pastors in the name of the Church." (*GS* 76)[16]

Pope John Paul II has enunciated the *communio* ecclesiology of the council, and developed its implications; he has deepened the commitment of Vat-

---

14 Cf. *Lumen Gentium*, §48–51; Pope John Paul II, *The Pope Speaks to the American Church* (New York: Harper, 1992), see the pages indexing the many aspects of *communio-koinonia* throughout all the pope's speeches; also Hermann J. Pottmeyer, *Unfehlbarkeit und Souveränität: Die Päpstliche Unfehlbarkeit im System der Ultramontanen Ekklesiologie des 19. Jahrhunderts* (Mainz: Matthias-Grünewald Verlag, 1975), 409–28.

15 *Gaudium et Spes* §76. The council continues to make clear that the differentiation is not a dualism or opposition between the eternal and the temporal.

16 Karol Wojtyla, *Sources of Renewal: The Implementation of Vatican II*, trans. P. S. Falla (New York: Harper & Row, 1980), 305, also 415–18.

ican II to evangelization.[17] This evangelization is directed both *ad gentes* and, at the same time, *ad intra,* to those who need to be strengthened in the faith, who need to understand better to live more genuinely the Catholic faith.

Whenever the Church deepens her differentiated understanding of the faith, there are those either who fail to embrace the *vetera* or who reject the *nova*. So, after Vatican II there are those who took up in new forms modernist orientations, and, at another extreme, those who see in the council betrayals of tradition. From the beginning of his papacy, John Paul II has insisted that the divisions in the Church, as well as those in the world, will only be healed and transcended by directing human minds and hearts toward Jesus Christ. Problems with the faith are always interpersonal problems between human persons and the Divine Persons. The new evangelization both *ad gentes* and *an intra* is not a matter of ecclesiastical politics or powerplays. It has to be rooted in a deepening life of prayer and faithful personal communion with the Risen Lord.

Orthodoxy is Grounded in the Reality of Christ

The *doctrina sana* or sound teaching of the Church's dogmatic and moral traditions are not just passing on "ideas" or "rules" or "symbols" on which Catholics are to think and guide their living. The sound and healing teachings of the Church are such because they mediate to us the Infinite Reality of the Triune God and the missions of the Word Incarnate and the Holy Spirit. As Thomas Aquinas emphasizes:

> Actus credendi non terminatur ad propositionem, sed ad rem; . . .
> Fides ergo facit hominem Deo inhaerere inquantum est nobis principium cognoscendi ver-itatem: credimus enim ea vera esse quae nobis a Deo dicuntur.[18]

True teachings, therefore, mediate to us the immediacy of the Triune God and the Risen Lord. As John Paul II states time and again in *Veritatis Splendor,* truth is not mere "ideas" but interpersonal discipleship even to

---

[17] Cf. Vatican II *Ad Gentes* §1–9; *Lumen Gentium* §1–8, 20, 48–51; commenting on Wojtyla's ecclesiology as expressed in his contributions to Vatican II, Kenneth Schmitz writes in his *At the Center of the Human Drama: The Philosophical Anthropology of Karol Wojtyla/Pope John Paul II* (Washington, DC: Catholic University of America Press, 1993), 109: "What is most telling from a philosophical perspective is his repeated insistence that all aspects of life are related to and grounded in the truth, and specifically in the truth embodied in, revealed by, and flowing from Christ."

[18] *Summa theologiae* II–II, q. 1, a. 2, ad 2; and q. 17, a. 6.

martyrdom. I see the mediation in truth of interpersonal immediacy as a leitmotif throughout the encyclical. Its opening sentences are clear:

> The splendor of truth shines forth in the works of the Creator and, in a special way, in man, created in the image and likeness of God (cf. Gen 1:26). Truth enlightens man's intelligence and shapes his freedom, leading him to know and love the Lord. Hence the Psalmist prays: "Let the light of your face shine on us, O Lord" (Ps 4:6). Called to salvation through faith in Jesus Christ, "the true light that enlightens everyone" (Jn 1:9), people become "light in the Lord" and "children of light" (Eph 5:8), and are made holy by "obedience to the truth" (1 Pet 1:22).[19]

The reference to the first letter of Peter is one that reveals well the mediated immediacy of the Word of God present in the teaching mission of the Church: Christ Jesus

> was chosen before the creation of the world, but was revealed in these last times for your sake. Through him you believe in God, who raised him from the dead and glorified him, and so your faith and hope are in God. Now that you have purified yourselves by obeying the truth so that you have sincere love for your brothers, love one another deeply, from the heart. For you have been born again, not of perishable seed, but of imperishable, through the living and enduring word of God. For, "All men are like grass, and all their glory is like the flowers of the field; the grass withers and the flowers fall, but the word of the Lord stands forever." And this is the word that was preached to you.[20]

The interpersonal immediacy mediated in true doctrine is again emphasized in the conclusion of *Veritatis Splendor* where the pope invokes Mary who received the true Word of God and continues to guide the faithful in the interpersonal fidelity to her Son: "No absolution offered by beguiling doctrines, even in the areas of philosophy and theology, can make man truly happy: only the Cross and the glory of the Risen Christ can grant peace to his conscience and salvation to his life."[21]

    This, of course, has been the orientation of the pope's evangelization effort from the very beginning. In doing this he continually calls our attention to the interpersonal dynamics of creation and redemption in

---

[19] *Veritatis Splendor,* intro. and 1.
[20] 1 Pet 1:20–25.
[21] *Veritatis Spendor* §120.

order to show how it is in Christ Jesus that the *vetera* and the *nova* are genuinely integrated.

John Paul II stated in his first encyclical, *Redemptor Hominis,* "the church's function in every age, and particularly in ours, is to direct man's gaze, to point the awareness and experience of the whole of humanity toward the mystery of God, to help all men to be familiar with the profundity of the Redemption taking place in Christ Jesus."[22] He is careful to point out how his emphasis upon the evangelization of cultures is simply carrying forward the catholic and apostolic mission of the church to preach the gospel to all peoples. He tells us that after two thousand years we are still only at the beginning of this mission of evangelization. He emphasizes how the process of evangelization depends upon a faithful discipleship of Christ, in which the law of the Cross, as lived out in the witness of the martyrs who gave up their life for the truth of the gospel, is paradigmatic for our own conversions. The Triune God's infinite wisdom chose to redeem humankind from evil, not by removing evil through divine power, but by transforming evil into good through the suffering, death, and resurrection of the Word Incarnate, Jesus Christ.[23]

What, then, is "new" about the evangelization efforts of Pope John Paul II? For one thing, the pope comes from an academic and philosophical background. No other modern pope had such an engagement with university teaching and no other modern pope has come to the papacy with such an extensive expertise in modern philosophy and phenomenological method. This has a profound influence on how he has fulfilled his magisterial responsibilities.[24] He has not hesitated to restate the ancient truth of Catholicism in categories with definite modern and postmodern lineage.

Take, for example, the above quotation from *Redemptor Hominis,* which he repeats in *Redemptoris Missio.* The Church's fundamental function is to direct man's gaze toward the mystery of Christ—this is standard Christian teaching from the time of the Apostles, bearing witness to the mission of the Word Incarnate in Christ Jesus. But the Holy Father says that this fundamental ecclesial function is "particularly" relevant to our age. He spells out just why it is. There are some theologians who call this fundamental ecclesial function into question:

---

[22] *Redemptor Hominis,* §10; also quoted in *Redemptoris Missio* §4.
[23] On the missiology of all Christian spirituality, cf. *Redemptoris Missio* §87–90
[24] There are, for example, annual meetings at Castel Gandolfo with intellectuals, most of them non-Catholics, for very free-ranging intellectual exchanges.

Is missionary work among non-Christians still relevant? Has it not been replaced by interreligious dialogue? Is not human development an adequate goal of the church's mission? Does not respect for conscience and for freedom exclude all efforts at conversion? Is it not possible to attain salvation in any religion? Why then should there be missionary activity?[25]

The modern age presents the church with the need to reaffirm its age-old mission of evangelization. Precisely because the modern age calls this mission into question, the teaching authority of the church must reaffirm it today.

John Paul II's Call for Catholic Wisdom as Ever Ancient and Ever New

There are those, especially those sympathetic to the theologians whom the pontiff is correcting, who view him as reversing the opening to the modern world supposedly begun at Vatican II.[26] Indeed, some conservatives, with very different evaluations, join liberals in seeing the present pope as dedicated to a type of restoration Catholicism.[27] Yet the only restoration John Paul II is committed to is the restoration of all things in Christ Jesus. He has embodied in his own life and ministry the only way in which Catholics and Christians can overcome the divisions that threaten so deeply the life of the Church. The unity of the Church is not a merely human accomplishment. It results from the missions of the Son and Spirit, it is pure and absolutely supernatural grace. All the political ideologies of right and left, of liberals and conservatives, do not go to the roots of the issues that divide them. For those roots spring from a twofold neglect: a failure to deepen one's union with the Triune God revealed in Christ through the Spirit, and a failure to understand adequately what John Paul II calls "the human dimension of the mystery of Redemption."[28] The pope continually calls attention to the divine and human interpersonal dimensions of the historical process of redemption.

This is how papal teachings avoid the extremes of liberalism, on the one hand, and restorationism or integralism, on the other hand. If the newness of the need for evangelization today partially consists in an "evan-

---

25 *Redemptoris Missio* §4.
26 Cf. Penny Lernoux, *People of God: The Struggle for World Catholicism* (New York: Penguin, 1986), where she criticizes Roman Restorationism under John Paul II.
27 Cf. Paul Johnson, *Pope John Paul II and the Catholic Restoration* (Ann Arbor, MI: Servant Books, 1981).
28 Cf. *Redemptor Hominis* §10.

gelization *ad intra*" because of the extent to which Catholics, including Catholic theologians, do not know and/or accept the teachings of the Catholic faith, the Holy Father continues to exhibit that deep strength of faith, so evident in the teachings of Vatican II, which does not hesitate to employ new categories he sees as capable of being helpful in articulating the wisdom ever ancient and ever new.

This can be illustrated from the same quotation. The pope takes a very ancient truth about how the mission of the church is to direct man's gaze toward the mystery of Christ and gives it a very modern formulation: This mission is "to point the awareness and experience of the whole of humanity toward the mystery of Christ."[29] To speak of the awareness and experience of the whole of humanity harkens back to the philosophical work of Karol Wojtyla. Just as consciousness is not left to idealist distortions, so experience is not left to empiricist or phenomenalist distortions. As studies on the pope's writings often state, the pope has a very unusual ability to bring together tradition and innovation, the ancient and the modern.[30]

The difficulties Catholicism has faced since the council (since, not because of) are rather massive. Roman Catholicism before Vatican II was viewed as the one remaining bulwark against modernity. The church was a large institutional presence in the Western world that had a quarrel with modernism in its various guises as liberalism, Americanism, socialism. For the "new" evangelization of John Paul II requires, among many other things, a theological and philosophical analysis of fundamental issues facing the church and the human race at the end of the second millennium of Christianity, to warn us against the "beguiling doctrines" referred to at the end of *Veritatis Splendor*.

The Effective History of Liberalism

It is erroneous to see in the pre-Vatican II Church only an undifferentiated rejection of modernity and liberalism. At times the use of social theoretical categories regarding the "subculture" of Roman Catholicism in the pre-Vatican II period fails to address the very real philosophical and theological contradictions between modernism and Catholicism.[31] Unless the dialectical

---

[29] John Paul II, *Redemptoris Missio* §1.

[30] Cf. Rocco Buttiglione, *Il Pensiero di Karol Wojtyla* (Milan: Jaca Books, 1982); George Williams, *The Mind of John Paul II* (New York: Seabury, 1981); Schmitz, *At the Center of the Human Drama*.

[31] For a more differentiated use, but still with too little attention, in my judgment, to philosophical and theological dialectics, cf. Joseph Komonchak, "Vatican II and the

differences are addressed with sufficient systematic analysis, one is liable to fall into a very undialectical social historicism. Beyond the historical question, if theologian *x* or *y* actually held a particular position condemned by Rome, there should be serious dialectical analysis to articulate the contradictory differences within the movements or cultural horizons in which theologian *x* or *y* lived and wrote.[32] From this dialectical perspective one can appreciate how the heresy of modernism, as well as Americanist principles and practices, do exhibit contradictions to Catholic faith and practice.

There is the notion, developed by Hans-Georg Gadamer, of *Wirkungsgeschichte* (effective history), which goes beyond the intentions of the individual historical agents to how, sometimes despite their intentions, movements de facto turn out.[33] Today we still are living the effective history of modernism and Americanism. This is evident not only in the popular culture but in the ongoing legal interpretations of the highest courts, as well as in the intellectual drift in a culture and theological writings more attuned with the drift than with Catholic theological traditions.[34]

Granted, there are differences between the traditions of Catholicism and liberalism that are complementary or genetic. Both liberals and neo-

---

Encounter Between Catholicism and Liberalism," in R. Bruce Douglass and David Hollenbach, eds., *Catholicism and Liberalism: Contributions to American Public Philosophy* (Cambridge: Cambridge University Press, 1994), 76–99. Again, in his "The Local Realization of the Church," in G. Alberigo, J.-P. Jossua, and J. Komonchak, eds., *The Reception of Vatican II* (Washington, DC: Catholic University of America Press, 1987), Komonchak speaks of the "collapse of Roman Catholicism" due to disappearance of what he terms a Catholic "sub-culture." Without attention to dialectics one is left—as I shall discuss with regard to Pelotte's work on John Courtney Murray—to envisage only an undifferentiated intransigence against modernity or an undifferentiated accommodation. A similar absence of dialectical philosophical and theological analysis hampers, in my judgment, David Tracy's analysis of pluralism in his *Plurality and Ambiguity* (New York: Crossroad, 1991).

32 On dialectical analysis, cf. Lonergan, *Method in Theology*, 235–66.

33 Cf. Hans-Georg Gadamer, *Truth and Method,* trans. Garrett Barden and John Cumming (New York: Seabury, 1975), 267ff., 305–25.

34 For examples of undifferentiated uses of sociological and political categories tending to collapse Catholicism into liberalism, cf. Dennis P. McCann, *New Experiment in Democracy: The Challenge for American Catholicism* (Kansas City: Sheed & Ward, 1987); Eugene C. Bianchi and Rosemary Ruether, eds., *A Democratic Catholic Church: The Reconstruction of Roman Catholicism* (New York: Crossroad, 1993). These books share the orientation of such as Edward Wakin and Joseph Scheuer, *The De-Romanization of the American Catholic Church* (New York: Macmillan, 1966) and John O'Connor, *The People Versus Rome: Radical Split in the American Church* (New York: Random House, 1969).

conservatives, for example, argue for complementary differences between Catholicism and liberalism in regard to human rights, the dignity of persons, the importance of voluntary communities, stewardship, entrepreneurship, and so on.[35] Such complementarity is usually spelled out in terms of a proper distinction of spheres or realms of the religious and the secular. Question arise about the complementarity. If one grants that neither the secular nor the sacred cancel one another, just how are they related? Indeed, complementarity covers a wide variety of positions.

Some seek to establish more genetic relationships between, for example, liberal human rights orientations and medieval discussions of natural rights.[36] Others argue for an American exceptionalism, seeing in Anglo-Saxon liberal

---

[35] Cf. Michael Novak, *Democracy and Mediating Structures: A Theological Inquiry.* (Washington, DC: American Enterprise Institute, 1980); idem, *The Spirit of Democratic Capitalism* (New York: Simon & Schuster, 1982); idem, *Free Persons and the Common Good* (Lanham, MD: Madison Books, 1989); George Weigel, *Tranquillitas Ordinis* (Oxford: Oxford University Press, 1987); idem, *Catholicism and the Renewal of American Democracy* (New York: Paulist Press, 1989); idem, "Is America Bourgeois?" *Crisis* 4 (October 1986): 5–10, and the controversy that ensued with David Schindler, cf. Mark Lowery, "The Schindler/Weigel Debate: An Appraisal," *Communio* 18 (1991): 425–72 with responses by Schindler and Weigel. Also David Schindler, "The Church's 'Worldly' Mission: Neoconservativism and American Culture," *Communio* 18 (1991): 365–97; Michael Novak, "Schindler's Conversion: The Catholic Right Accepts Pluralism," *Communio* 19 (1992): 145–78, with a response by David Schindler. On the liberal side, cf. David Hollenbach, *Justice, Peace and Human Rights* (New York: Crossroad, 1988); idem, "A Communitarian Reconstruction of Human Rights," in *Catholicism and Liberalism*, 127–50; John Coleman, *An American Strategic Theology* (New York: Paulist Press, 1982); David O'Brien, *Public Catholicism* (New York: Macmillan Publishing Company, 1989).

[36] Cf. Michel Villey, *La formation de la pensée juridique moderne,* 4th ed. (Paris: Aubier, 1975); Richard Tuck, *Natural Rights Theories: Their Origin and Development* (Cambridge: Cambridge University Press, 1979); Brian Tierney's following articles: "Tuck on Rights, Some Medieval Problems," *History of Political Thought* 4 (1983): 429–40; "Villey, Ockham and the Origin of Individual Rights," in *The Weightier Matters of the Law* (Atlanta: The American Academy of Religion, 1988), 1–31; "Conciliarism, Corporatism, and Individualism: the Doctrine of Individual Rights in Gerson," in *Cristianesimo nella storia* 9 (1988): 81–111; "Origins of Natural Rights Language: Texts and Contexts 1150–1250," *History of Political Thought* 10 (1989): 615–46; "Natural Rights in the Thirteenth Century" *Speculum* 67 (1992): 58–68. For a criticism of these presumed genetic relations, indicating how there are contradictory differences between medieval and modern notions of right, cf. Ernest Fortin, "On the Presumed Medieval Origin of Individual Rights" in his *Classical Christianity and the Political Order: Reflections on the Theologico-Political Problem* (Lanham, MD: Rowman & Littlefield, 1996), 243–64.

traditions antidotes to the secularism of continental European liberalism. Some argue this by claiming that John Locke and the American founders were committed to, or at least open to, genuine Christian orientations.

Without entering into these debates about complementarity and genetic relations, I would argue that the *Wirkungsgeschichte* of liberalism in the United States is hardly avoiding the pitfalls of classical liberalism. Those who seek to develop complementary and genetic contributions of liberalism to Catholicism would be aided by a dialectical discernment of those aspects of liberalism that contradict the truth of Catholic faith and practice. Not only that, but such a transformation of liberalism would aid its own development into a more just and good culture.

Effectively, hyper- or monadic individualism is pervasive. All human relationships tend to be viewed as merely contractual. The family is a greatly weakened and endangered institution. Just released census data indicate that 50 percent of all children in the United States live in families without the traditional biological mother and father. The subjectivism and rationalism of modernism is evident in how American culture portrays religion and reason. Religion is privatized, as a subjective emotion and opinion incapable of reasoned inquiry, while a rationalistic scientism seeks an objectivity that denies the reality of the human mind (e.g., cognitive science). If at the time of Leo XIII Americanism was extolling the natural virtues and forgetting the supernatural, it is now all too evident that the natural virtues have also been in drastic decline—as St. Augustine saw in the Roman culture of his day. The activism of American culture is all too evident, with a cultural aversion to the contemplative wisdom needed to attend to the wholeness of God's creation and how we as humans are called to intelligence, goodness, and holiness within this whole.

Liberalism without critical correctives becomes an ideology of sensate consumerism and very uncivil competitive individualism. John Gray indicates how the "domination of the American mind by liberal ideology has fostered blind spots in American perception of the real world that have been immensely disabling for policy," as well as for civility. The irony is that liberal ideology claims to be based on a universal tolerance, but, as Gray points out, it is becoming more intolerant in the name of conflicting rights.[37]

---

37 John Gray, *Post Liberalism: Studies in Political Thought* (New York: Routledge, 1993), 249ff.

The United States as Uniquely an Enlightenment Culture

Indeed, there is a particular and unique blend of classic European liberalism and modernism within the United States. The United States of America is the only fully Enlightenment and only fully "modern" state and culture on the globe. Canada did not revolt against the British monarch. No matter how modern the European, Asian, African, and Latin American states and cultures might be, only in the United States is there a national culture that can go back to a modern founding. Premodern memories came with the immigrants, but the country as such has no premodern cultural history except that of the Native Americans.

The *novus ordo seclorum* meant a strong break with the past. The new order was set up in stark opposition to, as a contradiction of, the old. In America both liberals and conservatives appealed to the same liberal founding and documents. Thus, conservatism in the United States has upheld the basic tenets of classic Anglo-Saxon and continental liberalism regarding the absolute rights of individuals, the privatization of religion, and a supposed impossibility of resolving the question of truth in serious disputes regarding morality and religion. So classic liberalism is blended with modernism in a peculiarly American fashion to the extent that no public or legal appeal can be made to premodern traditions.[38]

Clearly, it is time to revisit the Catholic condemnations of modernism and Americanism to more accurately reflect upon the dialectical differences between Catholicism and modernism/liberalism. The truly fundamental differences between them have not been resolved:[39] quite the contrary. The affirmation of religious liberty at Vatican II has, so to speak, cleared the deck for Catholicism to address the major errors of the intellectual traditions within modern liberalism. What *Dignitatis Humanae* did was to remove an appeal to coercion in matters of religious practice. But it did not ground the affirmation of religious freedom upon modernist or liberalist theories.

Instead, the council affirmed that the right of individuals and communities to religious freedom is "rooted in the social nature of man and in

---

[38] Cf. Mary Ann Glendon, *Abortion and Divorce in Western Law: American Failures and European Alternatives* (Cambridge: Harvard University Press, 1987); also her *Rights Talk: The Impoverishment of Political Discourse* (New York: Free Press, 1991) and *A Nation Under Lawyers* (New York: Farrar Straus, 1994).

[39] For a contrary assertion, cf. R Bruce Douglass's "Introduction" in *Catholicism and Liberalism*, 10.

the very nature of religion."[40] Indeed, the council repudiated modernist and liberal notions for "the right to religious freedom has its foundation not in the subjective attitude of the individual but in his very nature."[41] Analyzing divine faith, the council concluded:

> It is therefore fully in accordance with the nature of faith that in religious matters every form of coercion by men should be excluded. Consequently the principle of religious liberty contributes in no small way to the development of a situation in which men can without hindrance be invited to the Christian faith, embrace it of their own free will and give it practical expression in every sphere of their lives.[42]

Acknowledging mistakes made in the past, the council indicated that the principle of religious freedom harmonizes with the truth of God's creative and redemptive activity:

> The Church, therefore, faithful to the truth of the Gospel, is following in the path of Christ and the apostles when she recognizes the principle that religious liberty is in keeping with the dignity of man and divine revelation and gives it her support. Throughout the ages she has preserved and handed on the doctrine which she has received from her Master and the apostles. Although in the life of the people of God in its pilgrimage through the vicissitudes of human history there has at times appeared a form of behavior which was hardly in keeping with the spirit of the Gospel and was even opposed to it, it has always remained the teaching of the Church that no one is to be coerced into believing.[43]

The Unfinished Work of John Courtney Murray

To remove coercion explicitly and decisively at Vatican II was indeed, as Murray terms it, a recognition by the Church of a deeper historical "work of differentiation."[44] Unfortunately, Murray's commitment to the patient

---

[40] *Dignitatis Humanae* 4.
[41] Ibid., 2.
[42] Ibid., 10.
[43] Ibid., 12.
[44] John Courtney Murray, "The Declaration of Religious Freedom," 7–8. Work still needs to be done on Murray's use of dialectical method, and his use of Bernard Lonergan's writings. These are discussed, but not extensively analyzed, in Leon Hooper's *The Ethics of Discourse: The Social Philosophy of John Courtney Murray* (Washington, DC: Georgetown University Press, 1986). Hooper may accurately

intellectual work of thematizing the differentiations was cut short by his untimely death. The Catholic theological community in the United States has hardly excelled in carrying forward a concern for an intellectual differentiation of the issues involved in modernism and Americanism.[45] Instead, the theological issues were generally ignored or, as recently, there has been a theologically undifferentiated tendency to claim that modernism and Americanism was basically legitimated by Vatican II and that there ought to be a thorough reconstruction of Roman Catholicism along the lines of liberal democracy.[46] Rather than face the contradictory differences between Catholicism and modernism or Americanism, these theologians seek to "reconcile such contradictions" by playing down this or that Catholic teaching that goes against the grain of liberal cultures.[47]

Two problems confronting those who study Murray's contributions are, first, to measure up to his work of differentiation, and second, to articulate those aspects of liberalism that he did not study and so could not have foreseen the effective history of liberalism in the past three

---

portray Murray's use of dualism in regard to differentiation and the natural/supernatural distinction. If so it may indicate differences with Lonergan, as would also Hooper's failure to deal with the need in social philosophy for a theology of sin and redemption. Robert W. McElroy, *The Search for an American Public Theology: The Contribution of John Courtney Murray* (New York: Paulist Press, 1989) and Thomas P. Ferguson, *Catholic and American: The Political Theology of John Courtney Murray* (Kansas City: Sheed & Ward, 1993): Both provide general introductions, but do not take up more differentiated philosophical and theological questions.

45 On recent historical interest in Americanism, cf. Philip Gleason, "The New Americanism in Catholic Historiography," *U.S. Catholic Historian* 11 (1993): 1–18. The entire issue is devoted to the history of the condemnation of Americanism by Leo XIII, and contemporary efforts to construct a new Americanism.

46 Cf. note 33 above and references to McCann, Bianchi, and Ruether. There are also small organizations, such as the Association for Rights of Catholics in the Church, and so on, which publicly pressure Church authorities to accommodate to modern cultures without ever acknowledging that serious theological work is required. A case in point is the ordination of women. To date only two Catholic theologians have written books on this question, both in German, with one pro and the more recent and thorough being contra. No North American theologian has published an in-depth study of the issue. Instead, the Catholic Theological Society of America and College Theology Society treat it as a political right of women, all part of the great American drive for unisex equality. Priesthood is seen as conferring power and status contrary to motherhood and celibacy.

47 On the link between modernism and Americanism, cf. Gene Burns, *The Frontiers of Catholicism: The Politics of Ideology in a Liberal World* (Berkeley: University of California Press, 1992); R. Scott Appleby, *Church and Age Unite! The Modernist Impulse in American Catholicism* (Notre Dame, IN: University of Notre Dame Press, 1992).

decades. Murray did not engage, as far as I can determine, in a detailed study of Hobbes, Hume, and Locke, and their impact on the American founding. This is why it is important to attend to the dialectical differences between Catholicism and liberalism.

Those studying Murray have sometimes failed to present the dialectics of differentiation as carefully as he did. Donald E. Pelotte's study of Murray has the theologian basically arguing for a complementarity of Catholicism and liberalism, along with some genetic relations of Anglo-Saxon liberal rights language and medieval schoolmen.[48] He does not attend sufficiently to the dialectic Murray, and most certainly Vatican II, discerned in the process of secularist liberalism within the United States.[49] It is not surprising, therefore, that the final chapter places Murray within the "Americanist Tradition." Pelotte wrongly sees the only alternatives for the Catholic Church in America as either assimilation or separation:

> The Americanist crisis involved the question of the extent to which the Church should enter the mainstream of American political, economic, and social life. She could do either of two things: accept wholeheartedly "Americanization," the assimilation of immigrants into the American culture, embrace the American life and its institutions, or remain aloof and adopt an attitude of cultural separation and protectionism.[50]

This overlooks precisely that the dialectical task is to avoid both wholehearted assimilation and aloof separation. Framing Americanism in this way assures that the dialectical contributions of Murray are overlooked, and Murray is ironically portrayed as an Americanist.

Reading *Testem Benevolentiae* today, one cannot but see how it is a pastoral plea for a dialectical discernment in the relations between Catholicism and American culture, rather than either an aloof separation or wholehearted assimilation. The warnings on subjectivist piety, eschewing the external mediations of the Church, the downplaying of the theo-

---

48 Donald E. Pelotte, *John Courtney Murray: Theologian in Conflict* (New York: Paulist Press, 1976). For example, Pelotte on page 122 writes that "Murray considered the American Constitution and the American political system the best exemplification of the modern political development of the lay democratic state," whereas he quotes Murray on page 159 showing how Murray was quite aware of the ambiguities and defects in the American political system.

49 Ibid., 115–40: chapter four, "Murray's American Political Philosophy."

50 Ibid., 147.

logical virtues in favor of natural human abilities, the confusion of license for liberty, the naive trust in democracy to determine by consensus good and evil, the universalizing of American experience and expertise—these are hardly non-existent tendencies. Little wonder that Pelotte's undifferentiated treatment of Murray would be appealed to by those who find modernism and Americanism important in their "reconstructions" of Roman Catholicism as a "participatory democracy" or "enterprising spirit" that would not only reconstruct the Church but also reinvigorate the naked public square of the nation.[51]

Dialectical Differences between Catholicism and Liberalism

In order to transform modern and liberal cultures through the Gospel of Jesus Christ it would be helpful to understand the major dialectical differences between Catholicism and the philosophical and theological implications of modernism or Americanism. Because Murray did not conduct a careful philosophical and theological analysis of Thomas Hobbes, David Hume, and John Locke, as well as their influence on the American founding, his arguments for American exceptionalism and an Anglo-Saxon difference need to be further differentiated.[52]

I shall briefly discuss four major differences. The point about these dialectical differences is that the contradictions to the truth of Catholic faith are also contradicting the dynamic orientations of human nature and the orientation of the whole created order of the universe. Murray's efforts to recognize the importance of natural law, and the need for developing arguments that appeal to human reason, have to be recovered and further differentiated.[53] These dialectical differences do not cancel out the contributions modern cultures and America make to human development, such as the marvelous expansion of the empirical sciences, new technologies,

---

[51] Cf. Dennis McCann, *New Experiment in Democracy*; on the inadequacy of these appeals to Americanism, cf. William Portier, "Inculturation as Transformation: The Case of Americanism Revisited," *U.S. Catholic Historian* 11 (1993): 107–24, especially 109–11.

[52] Cf. Keith J. Pavlischek, *John Courtney Murray and the Dilemma of Religious Toleration* (Lanham, MD: Thomas Jefferson University Press, 1994).

[53] Cf. Alasdair MacIntyre, *Three Rival Traditions of Moral Enquiry* (Notre Dame, IN: University of Notre Dame Press, 1990); Daniel Mark Nelson, *The Priority of Prudence: Virtue and Natural Law in Thomas Aquinas and the Implications for Modern Ethics* (University Park, PA: The Pennsylvania State University Press, 1992).

exchange economies capable of growth, political dedication to human dignity, and responsible freedom. Indeed, the following contradictions between Catholicism and liberalism not only make it difficult for Catholic faith to flourish, but also the contradictions hamper the proper development of human reason and political responsibility in modern cultures.

All of these dialectical contradictions are shared by all sides within modern cultures; none are unique to one side or the other in the usual modern debates. The philosophical and theological implications of modernism and Americanism are shared by liberals, conservatives, and radicals. They could be documented in most if not all of the major figures in the development of modern cultures.[54]

The Loss of Revelation and the Alienation of Human Reason

Fundamental to the contradictions between Catholicism and modernity is an effort at the base of modern post-Enlightenment cultures: first to do away with revealed religion in the name of a God more reasonable, and then to do away with God in the name of reason. This process of two-step secularism is deeply imbedded in American culture.[55] Without revelation and the theological virtues, modernity was fated to retrace in its own way the decline that undid Greco-Roman cultures. Bereft of the light of faith, human reason can make sense of nature and history only by reading sin and evil into the cosmos and human nature. Without revelation and faith there is no notion of sin and redemption, and so evil and death become either illusory or all-consuming.

St. Augustine analyzed this in Book Nineteen of the *City of God.* Those who had acquired the intellectual and moral virtues were unable to avoid a stoic withdrawal from suffering and/or a cynical retreat from understanding. Stoicism and cynicism accompanied the descent of Rome into a sensate foolishness. Only Catholic faith in the Incarnate Word of God enlightened one to both the intrinsic goodness of God's creation, the introduction of evil by the sins of intelligent free creatures, and the supernatural restoration of goodness by the redemptive life, death, and resurrec-

---

54 Cf. chapter 6 below.

55 Cf. James Turner, *Without God, Without Creed: The Origins of Unbelief in America* (Baltimore: John Hopkins University Press, 1985); Lonergan traces this process as a longer cycle of decline in *Insight*, 250–67, especially 254: "Culture retreats into an ivory tower. Religion becomes an inward affair of the heart. Philosophy glitters like a gem with endless facets and no practical purpose." Also on the fundamental importance of theology for the human sciences, see 753–70.

tion of the Word Incarnate in Christ Jesus. Augustine realized that Roman culture was in such serious decline that all his efforts should be directed at living out the mission of the Church in building up the city of God. Without revealed faith, Augustine saw the reign of the *summum malum* of warfare and death; only Christ reveals the *summum bonum* of the eternal peace of the ordered totality of creation and redemption.[56]

Centuries later St. Thomas Aquinas would grasp the systematic significance of this process and develop how the theological virtue of agapic love informs all other virtues. Without theological virtues, moral virtues, unable to attain the true end of graced beatitude, cannot long sustain the trials of human living. The decline of moral virtues leads to the decline of practical wisdom, while the lack of the gift of wisdom leaves science and philosophy unenlightened as to the whole process of the *exitus* of creation from God, the fall of intelligent creatures through sin, and the *reditus* of the universe back to God in redemption.[57]

The Enlightenment in both its continental and Anglo-Saxon forms lost the enlightenment that faith provides. Machiavelli rejected the ancient wisdom, the cultivation of the virtues, as impractical in the power politics of his day. *Virtù* would now be the cunning use of religion and the appearance of virtue in order for the prince to maintain power at all costs. Not the kingdom of God but the reign of the prince became the ultimate end of the city of man.[58]

What Machiavelli did for the prince, Hobbes extended to all the citizens. There is no wise mediation of the whole of reality, no praise for the harmonious symphony of creation and mankind's place in it. The whole is dissolved in violence and the *bellum omnium contra omnes*. Nature is a hostile environment against which man must defend himself by his science and technology. Force and fraud, fear and violence are the marks of human history. The revealed story of original paradise is transmuted into a "state of nature" where violence and war are supreme. The first modern affirmation of the equality of all men was made in just such a context. Because "all men in the state of nature have a desire and will to hurt" one another,

---

[56] St. Augustine, *The City of God,* Book XIX, chapters 6–28, especially 12, 14, 15, 25.

[57] *Summa theologiae* I–II, qq. 58, 65; II–II, q. 23, aa. 45–46.

[58] Machiavelli, *The Prince,* trans. Mark Musa (New York: St. Martin's Press, 1964), chapters 6, 15–19.

> the cause of mutual fear consists partly in the natural equality of
> men, partly in their mutual will of hurting. . . . Even the weakest
> man can kill the strongest, so . . . they are equals who can do equal
> things one against the other.[59]

Instead of a metaphysics of being, Hobbes developed a metamechanics of
nature, both physical, human, and of the body politic. Given the violence
of the state of nature, all we have is isolated individual beings; any and all
ways of patterning or ordering them are impositions on them. Law is not
an education in natural orientations toward goodness but an act of power
mechanically ordering the automata of otherwise discordant elements. All
knowledge and science is born of fear.[60]

Catholicism, along with Judaism, offers a very different orientation.
God's creative act is not an act of violence and domination—indeed, the
Hebrew creation narratives repudiated the violent cosmogonies of the surrounding empires. The empires and superpowers of history have become
what they are through force and violence so it is hardly surprising that
their visions of world birth would be violent. Quite different are the narratives of chosen people and the disciples of Jesus. Creation is good, creation nourishes us and metaphors of gardening, not killing, are central.
Indeed, Catholic faith reveals how the whole of reality is ultimately interpersonal. The Triune God speaks and the universe comes into being. Created persons come into being and are called to respond in faith and love to
one another and the Triune God. Violence and force enter, not in nature
but in the free refusal of these persons to respond to God's love. Even
though all are descendents of Cain, God still loves us and redeems us first
through the covenant with Israel and finally by sending his only Son.[61]

An ontology of conflict and violence underlying modernism is linked
with the emergence of the nation-states, including the United States.[62]
The loss of theology as an integral part of knowledge, the complete severance of all science from wisdom, the purported end of metaphysics—all

59 Thomas Hobbes, *De Cive or the Citizen,* trans. S. Lamprecht (New York: Apple-
   ton, 1947), chapter 1.
60 Thomas Hobbes, *The Leviathan,* ed. C. B. MacPherson (New York: Pelican Classics, 1976), 81–216.
61 *RH* §7–8.
62 Cf. Anthony Giddens, *The Nation State and Violence* (Berkeley: University of California Press, 1989); Bruce D. Porter, *War and the Rise of the State: The Military
   Foundations of Modern Politics* (New York: Free Press, 1994).

contribute to a loss of the sense of the whole. This is intensified by the veritable explosion of the empirical sciences, specializing in the empirical investigations of all aspects of the world and life. A Catholic understanding of the intrinsic relation between the light of reason and the light of faith demands a collaborative relation between the sciences and theology. As John Paul II has written:

> Only a dynamic relationship between theology and science can reveal those limits which support the integrity of either discipline, so that theology does not profess pseudo-science and science does not become an unconscious theology. Our knowledge of each other can lead us to be more authentically ourselves. No one can read the history of the past century and not realize that crisis is upon us both. The uses of science have on more than one occasion proven massively destructive, and the reflections on religion have too often been sterile. We need each other to be what we must be, what we are called to be.[63]

Given sin and the massive injustices in human history, the importance of holiness and the theological virtues cannot be overestimated in the tasks of a new wisdom-oriented evangelization. The fact that theology has disappeared from the cultural patrimony of our modern and American intellectual establishments has meant that empirical science is bereft of the wisdom it so desperately needs (the empirical sciences are charting how human beings behave, how they act). They are ascribing that behavior—no matter how violent and sinful it is—to human nature. On the basis of such studies social policies are formulated, and so the violence and sin becomes structured into the society and culture.

In such cycles of social and cultural decline the intellectually virtuous tend toward cynicism, while the morally virtuous tend toward stoicism. The intelligent quest for wisdom and science, as well as the moral quest for justice, should not succumb to cynicism and indifference. Because our kingdom is not of this world, we can dedicate ourselves to the creative and redemptive transformation of this world. Because through faith, hope, and love we are in communion with the absolutely transcendent Triune God, we are members of one another in the historically immanent mediations of the missions of the Word and the Spirit to bring about the Kingdom of God in

---

[63] *John Paul II on Science and Religion: Reflections on the New View from Rome* (Vatican: Vatican Observatory Publications, 1990), 14.

our time and culture. It is only in the context of hope in the transcendent Kingdom of God that the healing and creating tasks of building a truly good life immanent within the world can continue in the face of evil and decline. A proper theological understanding of the theorem of the supernatural elaborated by Thomas Aquinas is critical in developing the implications of the differentiation of sacred and secular, of faith and reason.[64]

Loss of Whole and Hyper-Individualism

Another dialectical difference between Catholicism and modernism flows from the first: the hyper- or monadic individualism in modern cultures. Without a grasp of the whole of creation as oriented toward the goodness, truth, and holiness of the Triune God, modern thinkers have tended to view all phenomena as monadic, to use Leibniz's term. The empirical sciences concentrated upon individual things. Nominalism had prepared the way for this.[65] As physical monads are viewed as existing in fields of force and counterforce, so human monads are seen as endowed with prepolitical rights as a kind of armor that they have to use in the struggle for existence. All natural and human orders—the relationships between the monads—are conceived as imposed on the monads by dominative power. If the present power relations are not to one's advantage, then the task is to band together into pressure groups in order to gain what one believes are one's rights. For moderns there is no whole that can be heuristically known in a critically grounded metaphysics, because for it only individuals exist. Then there is no way of mediating the natural created order in which each thing exists, there is no sense of nature as a whole. All relations tend to be conceived as extrinsic.

As John Paul II points out, the natural sciences are beginning to move beyond the nominalist hyper-individualism of modernism. On the one side, there is the growing need for interdisciplinary collaboration among the individual sciences as more and more internal relations among things are seen as important. On the other side, the growing concern for environmental health is restoring a sense of nature as a whole. In both movements, Catholicism has much to contribute to reversing the counterpositions of modernism.[66]

---

[64] Cf. Bernard Lonergan, *Grace and Freedom: Operative Grace in the Thought of St. Thomas Aquinas,* ed. P. Burns (New York: Herder & Herder, 1971); Michael Stebbins, *The Divine Initiative* (Toronto: University of Toronto Press, 1994).

[65] Cf. Dupré, *Passage to Modernity,* 80–88, 176–208.

[66] Cf. John Paul II, *On Science and Religion*; also the social teachings of all the modern popes.

This hyper-individualism in the political and cultural spheres will not be easily healed. Individualist rights talk and practice is widespread. This individualist rights (dis)orientation in modernism and Americanism ignores nature completely. Indeed, the individualist ethics argues only from individual cases. Taking a cue from seventeenth-century casuists, Thomas Hobbes and the modernists after him used extreme individual cases around which they would build their political and moral theories: For example, the case of Robinson Crusoe becomes paradigmatic for individuals in a "state of nature" endowed with prepolitical rights, engaged in a life-and-death struggle for existence. The exceptions become the norm, so all norms disappear.[67]

Catholic social teaching has shown its dialectical strength in these matters. It does not reject rights language, but incorporates it within a philosophical context that rejects the nominalism and hyper-individualism of any notion of prepolitical rights.[68] The wholistic context of Catholic use of rights categories emphasizes how the dignity of the human person is within the context of the gift of creation and redemption in which each human person is created in the image and likeness of the Triune God. Moreover, there has been since John Paul II a much greater emphasis upon solidarity.[69] The importance of solidarity as a way of transforming political and cultural monadic individualism demands attention to a recovery of a metaphysics of human solidarity, as well as an ethics and a theology.[70]

This is especially important for the United States as the social, legal, and cultural implications of hyper-individualism are wreaking havoc on the unborn, on children, on the family, and on the sick and old. Recent court decisions are indices of the disintegration of our society and culture. Thus the Supreme Court 1992 decision in *Planned Parenthood* v. *Carey* provides a monadic definition of freedom: "At the heart of liberty is the right to define one's own concept of existence, of meaning, of the universe, and of the mystery of human life." This then provided the premise for a decision

---

[67] Cf. Mary Ann Glendon, *Rights Talk*; Ernest Fortin, *Human Rights, Virtue, and the Common Good: Untimely Meditations on Religion and Politics* (Lanham, MD: Rowman & Littlefield, 1996).

[68] Cf. Jean Bethke Elshtain, "Relationship of Public and Private," in *The New Dictionary of Catholic Social Thought* (Collegeville MN: The Liturgical Press, 1994), 795ff.; also her "Judge Not?" in *First Things* (46; October 1994): 36–40.

[69] John Paul II, *Laborem Exercens; Solititude Rei Socialis; Centesimus Annus*.

[70] Cf. Matthew Lamb, "Solidarity," in *The New Dictionary of Catholic Social Thought*, 908–12.

by Judge Barbara Rothstein, in the U.S. District Court in the State of Washington to decide in favor of a right to physician-assisted suicide:

> However, this court finds the reasoning in *Casey* highly instructive and almost prescriptive on this latter issue [regarding the question of what liberty interest may inhere in a terminally ill person's choice to commit physician-assisted suicide]. . . . Thus consonant with the reasoning in *Casey*, such an intimate personal decision falls within the realm of the liberties constitutionally protected under the 14th Amendment.[71]

John Paul II spells out these hazards of individualistic ethics in striking clarity:

> Certain currents of modern thought have gone so far as to *exalt freedom to such an extent that it becomes an absolute, which would then be the source of values.* This is the direction taken by doctrines which have lost the sense of the transcendent or which are explicitly atheistic. The individual conscience is accorded the status of a supreme tribunal of moral judgment which hands down categorical and infallible decisions about good and evil. To the affirmation that one has a duty to follow one's conscience is unduly added the affirmation that one's moral judgment is true merely by the fact that it has its origin in the conscience. But in this way the inescapable claims of truth disappear, yielding their place to a criterion of sincerity, authenticity and "being at peace with oneself," so much so that some have come to adopt a radically subjectivistic conception of moral judgment.
>
> As is immediately evident, *the crisis of truth* is not unconnected with this development. Once the idea of a universal truth about the good, knowable by human reason, is lost, inevitably the notion of conscience also changes. Conscience is no longer considered in its primordial reality as an act of a person's intelligence, the function of which is to apply the universal knowledge of the good in a specific situation and thus to express a judgment about the right conduct to be chosen here and now. Instead, there is a tendency to grant to the individual conscience the prerogative of independently determining the criteria of good and evil and then acting accordingly. Such an outlook is quite congenial to an individualistic ethic, wherein each individual is faced with his own truth, different from the truth of others. Taken to its extreme consequences, this individualism leads to a denial of the very idea of human nature.

---

[71] John Paul II, *VS* §32. Cf. his *The Acting Person* (New York: Springer-Verlag, 1979), 136ff.

These different notions are at the origin of currents of thought which posit a radical opposition between moral law and conscience, and between nature and freedom.[72]

John Paul II emphasizes how we need to recover a deeper understanding of the natural law, and to realize how the Catholic tradition on law situates law within the context of education into the good. Law is not to be an isolated act of the will commanding arbitrarily, but an act informed with practical wisdom. The importance of what the pope in *Veritatis Splendor* terms "moral conscience" and the tradition called *"prudentia"* is central to avoid both an objectivism in law that excludes human agency and a subjectivism that excludes truth and objective moral absolutes.[73]

Loss of Wisdom and the Modern Eclipse of Judgment—Truth

As the loss of the whole, the *kaq olon* that Catholic literally means, leads to a monadic individualism, so this individualism leads to an eclipse of judgment and truth in modernism and Americanism. Knowledge is equated with power, and the eclipse of judgment leaves modern cognitional theories and epistemologies with only categories of experience and thinking, on the cognitive side, and categories of deliberation and decision, on the volitional side. Of all the experiences and ideas one has, which are true? Without attention to the dynamics of judgment-mediating experience and thought by discovering which are true to reality and which false, moderns wrongly envisage truth as an arbitrary decision. This is true because someone in power decided it was true.

Wisdom is lost to the demands of dominative power, as the works of Michel Foucault document. Knowledge in this context is generated by fear. The cognitional theoretical investigations of Karol Wojtyla and Bernard Lonergan make clear that the Cartesian subjectivism of the *ego cogito* so exalts "thinking" that it fails to attend to what Augustine and Aquinas termed "understanding," and so broke the intrinsic relationship between understanding and the judgment of truth.[74] Knowledge is born, not of fear,

---

[72] See the decision rendered by Judge Rothstein's decision *Compassion in Dying* v. *Washington*, 850 F. Supp. 1454, 1460 (W. D. Washington 1994).

[73] Cf. *VS* §54–64; also Nelson, *The Priority of Prudence.*

[74] Cf. Karol Wojtyla, *The Acting Person,* 124–63, 303, 306; Bernard Lonergan, *Verbum: Word and Idea in Aquinas,* ed. D. Burrell (Notre Dame, IN: University of Notre Dame Press, 1968), 47–95; also his *Insight,* 304–409, 413–14.

but of a love of wisdom and understanding. In the Catholic tradition truth has never been a category of dominative power but of wisdom. On the other side, there is the romantic emotivism that promotes the subjectivism so rampant in new age spirituality and the Rousseau's "animal sympathy" or amoral compassion in modernism and Americanism.[75] A recovery of Catholic wisdom is desperately needed in contemporary modern and American cultures, as the receptions of *Veritatis Splendor* and the new Catechism highlight.

Institutions as Patterns of Domination or Cooperation?

The above three dialectical differences flow into a major difference between modernism and Catholicism regarding institutions. Within modernism and Americanism there is the tendency to view institutions as organizational structures that are purely voluntary and impose an order on the individual members because they all agree to work for some common goal. This view of institutions was laid out in great detail by Max Weber, who sees them as *Herrschaftsstrukturen* or structures of domination. The key is to have legitimate dominative structures, and for us moderns, Weber concluded, legitimacy was by the choice of the majority. This refined Rousseau's "social contract" approach and, through Talcott Parsons, has become standard (even thought Parsons left out "domination" when describing them) in Western sociology.

It is evident how this theory and practice of institutions fits in with a conflictual approach to reality, a hyper-individualism, and the notion that knowledge is power. The individual is viewed as giving up some aspect of his or her freedom by joining an institution in order to work together with the others. Social and cultural institutions are structures of legitimate domination whereby monadic individuals more or less agree to the forms of legitimate coercion (legal force and fear) required to establish and maintain the conventional orders of enlightened society.[76] Within this context, freedom is freedom to pursue one's own individual self-interest. Freedom is basically value-neutral, for any supra-individual norm is taken as no more than conventional, and so imposed either by dictate or by consensus. There are only, then, procedural norms—no substantiative norms—for

---

75 Cf. Leo Strauss, *An Introduction to Political Philosophy*, 51–57, 89–93; Stanley Hauerwas, "Killing Compassion," in his *Dispatches from the Front* (Durham, NC: Duke University Press, 1994), 164–76.

76 Cf. Leo Strauss, *The Political Philosophy of Hobbes: Its Basis and Its Genesis*, trans. E. Sinclair (Chicago: University of Chicago Press, 1984); the work of Hobbes influenced F. Tönnies, who in turn influenced Max Weber.

what is good. Hence the distinction between legality and morality is a distinction without a difference. The instrumentalization of nature, life, and society proceeds apace. Any institution that is not voluntary is looked down upon, for example, the family, since individuals are portrayed as primordially solitary rather than, as in Catholicism and premodern cultures, as being naturally social and communal.

In Catholic traditions, institutions are primarily patterns of cooperation through which the common good is known and effected. There is no prepolitical state of nature in which we have isolated monadic individuals; rather human beings are naturally social and political. Freedom, therefore, is not value-neutral but oriented toward the truly good. Freedom is intrinsically, by our very created natures, normed toward a happiness in the truly good in community with others. Institutions, when they function as they should, do not restrict our freedom but enable it to maturely attain the good. As long as our desires are properly ordered, as we choose the good, our freedom expands. Insofar as our desires are disordered, and we choose evil, our freedom contracts. Institutional laws and regulations are not instrumental, aimed at imposing arbitrary orders, but are to be fundamentally educative in the good.

Conclusion

A theology of institutions would develop how they are meant to share in the Eucharistic orientation of all of human life. Catholicism has many resources to bring to modern and American cultures with its sense of community as fundamental to all social institutions. Catholics have learned some important lessons in respect of individuals from modern cultures. In our tradition institution and community, as well as community and individual, are not juxtaposed but intrinsically defined by each other. Institutional authority is as different from authoritarianism as love making is from rape. The treasure of Catholic teachings on discernment and authority in the service of building up the Church and a culture of love needs to be both recovered and lived. Fundamental also is Catholic teaching and practice on the family. Theologically, just as the Triune God is more intimate to each individual than that individual is even to himself or herself, so that incredible individual intimacy is universal. As individuals we are all intrinsically related to others. There is no autobiography that is not ipso facto also a heterobiography. We are all members one of another. Family is a natural community, so we move from it to the supernatural family of God. One is the gift of creation, the other the gift of redemption.

There is much work for Catholic theologians to do as we revisit, more dialectically than we have in the past, modernism and Americanism.

CHAPTER 6

Inculturation and Western Culture: The Dialogical Experience Between Gospel and Culture

MY TASK HERE is to provide some systematic theological reflections on the process of inculturation. The title and subtitle are rather daunting. Who is the subject for "the dialogical experience between the Gospel and Culture?" "Western culture" would be, to quote Gandhi, a wonderful idea.

Christianity is certainly integral to any understanding of Western cultures. To address the issues involved in the topic requires attention to certain transcultural achievements in Catholic theology. For the subject of "the dialogical experience" is nothing less than the whole Christ, Head and members.

By way of opening our discussions, I shall specify two interrelated sets of topics: (1) inculturation and the transcultural; and (2) Catholic theological resources for inculturation. Finally, I shall conclude by posing some questions regarding inculturating the Catholic faith in U.S. culture.

Inculturation and the Transcultural

By way of introduction, I should mention how we ought to be careful when speaking of "culture." It is a typically modern notion. Very often it is separated from "nature" and, if we are not careful, we can fall into a Cartesian or Kantian way of viewing both nature and culture as if we were spectators. For Augustine and Aquinas nature embraces both material natures

This essay was originally published as "Inculturation and Western Culture" in *Communio: International Catholic Review* XXI (1; Spring 1994): 124–44.

and spiritual natures like human minds, angels, and God. The human mind is most divine in us, and the image of God in us, has a nature. There are patterns or natural ordered orientations of human experiencing, understanding, judging, deciding, loving, and acting that we do not make up, they are from nature. We either follow the natural order or pattern within our rational nature, or we fail to live as genuinely as human beings ought to live. The human mind and soul transcend all particular cultures. Our minds are not just the sum of all the things that we have learned in our particular culture. Wisdom attends to these transcultural patterns and ordered orientations. This is why any historicism or cultural relativism is simply wrong—a too typically modern eclipse of wisdom and the human mind. The mind is much more than a Cartesian "thinking thing." The more ancient approach to nature and mind is what leads John Paul II to refer to how "there is only one culture: that of man and for man."[1]

Cultural anthropology uses the term "inculturation" to designate the learning process by which individuals and communities are assimilated into a culture. "Socialization" is also used for this learning process; but it may be helpful to distinguish between society as the complex of organizations aimed at procuring the goods of life (technologies and economies geared toward regularly procuring particular goods such as food, shelter, etc.) and culture as the pattern of beliefs, meanings, and values that imply or define what the good life is for those in the culture. The cultural goes beyond or transcends the social. Similar social organizations may have very different cultural patterns (e.g., socially both Japan and the U.S. have high technology exchange economies, but the cultures are very different). There is the question of just how independent a culture is from the social infrastructure, and the extent to which global technologies and economies are in fact homogenizing cultures.

The process of inculturation, then, involves both the learning process and what is learned. There are the individuals and communities who learn, and by learning come to live and know their culture. The distinction between the learning and what is learned is most important, for cultures are not static, immutable things. Cultures change depending upon how well or poorly they are learned. Nor is the learning merely receptive, it can also be creative as the culture is gradually or abruptly changed by new meanings, values, beliefs. Creative individuals and communities can

---

[1] Cf. The Apostolic Constitution *Ex Corde Ecclesiae* §3. Also the attention to truth and natural law in his *Veritatis Splendor*.

change the culture so that the living it promotes is better than it was, just as unintelligent individuals and communities bring about cultural disintegration and decay.

Theological uses of "inculturation" are relatively recent.[2] The specifically theological use of the term, especially in ecclesial and papal documents, refers to the process of how the Church, mediating the proclamation of the Gospel, is involved in a mutual learning process wherein the Gospel is received and, in that very reception, brings about over time transformations of the particular culture and new "incarnations" of the Church. Fr. Crollius summarizes the process as follows:

> . . . the inculturation of the Church is the integration of the Christ-
> ian experience of a local Church into the culture of its people, in
> such a way that this experience not only expresses itself in elements
> of this culture, but becomes a force that animates, orients and inno-
> vates this culture so as to create a new unity and communion, not
> only with the culture in question but also as an enrichment of the
> Church universal.[3]

This process of ecclesial inculturation is not completely *sui generis* in the sense that there is no *praeparatio evangelii* within the processes studied by cultural anthropologists, social psychologists, and political theorists. The Gospel provides a higher viewpoint within which to create, heal, and transform cultures. But we have already seen how culture itself is a higher viewpoint in regard to the technological and economic processes constitutive of the social.

A major reason for a renewed theological interest in the process of inculturation is precisely to avoid what I would call extrinsic absolutism, on the one extreme, and an equally extrinsic relativism at the other extreme. Extrinsic absolutism is an error that identifies the absolute truth and normativeness of the Gospel with extrinsic, finite words or ideas, and it takes at least two forms. One form is a fundamentalist literalism, whether as that found among the Arians of the fourth century, who rejected the Nicean *homousion*

---

[2] Cf. Ary A. Roest Crollius, ed., *Inculturation and the Challenges of Modernity* (Rome: Gregorian, 1982); idem, *What is So New about Inculturation?* (Rome: Gregorian, 1984); Peter Schineller, ed., *On Being Church in a Modern Society* (Rome: Gregorian, 1983); and the other volumes in the Gregorian series of working papers on inculturation; Francis George, *Inculturation and Ecclesial Communion: Culture and Church in the Teachings of Pope John Paul II* (Rome: Urbaniana, 1990).

[3] *What is So New about Inculturation?*, 15–16.

because it was not found in the Bible, or our contemporary fundamentalists for whom the only thing required for inculturating the Gospel is to translate it into a relevant language. Another form of extrinsic absolutism can be found in the "essentialists" who seek to distill into propositional form the "essence" of the Gospel as if this essence would then reside in some conceptually pure realm and could be planted in any culture and sprout.

Inadequate reactions to this extrinsic absolutism then tend to swing over into a rejection of any and all absolutes. Because the fundamentalists and essentialists lack the wisdom to know how the Divine Truth is present in the ordering of creation and the redemption of history, those who criticize them without adverting themselves to that wisdom tend toward a relativism. They imagine that any discussion of absolutes is at bottom no more than an exercise of power, and so they opt for a multiculturalism without absolutes or any intrinsic intelligibility within the Gospel message. Sometimes any discussion of the absolute demands of the faith, and the need for transcultural mediations of Church and sacrament, are dismissed as "colonialism."[4]

Two forms this relativism takes are syncretism and parallelism. In both the culture in fact becomes normative for the faith. In syncretism there is a "mixture or amalgamation of belief systems" that in fact truncates the Gospel by attending only to the mixing of extrinsic beliefs and practices; no vital unity and communion results.[5] Parallelism keeps the diverse systems of beliefs and practices separate, but still truncates the Spirit of the Gospel since no genuine unity or communion, and so no genuine inculturation, really occurs.

The use of inculturation, then, is meant precisely to avoid the extrinsicism or what may be called the *fallacy of misplaced normativeness* underlying essentialism, fundamentalism, syncretism, and parallelism. The absolute normativity of the Gospel is the concrete Person of Jesus Christ, the Word Incarnate, as sent by the Father and with the Father sending the Spirit to inform the ongoing mission of the Church to proclaim the Gospel and make disciples of all nations. To understand how this absolute and concrete normativeness functions, it is important to understand how the religious grounds the cultural, and how the Triune God creates and redeems the religious.

---

4 Many discussions of evangelization and colonialism fall into a genealogist perspective in which truth is misunderstood as just another manifestation of dominative power.

5 Cf. George, *Inculturation and Ecclesial Communion*, 221ff., and references given there.

Any genuine culture also inculturates a transcultural orientation to the religious. We have seen how the cultural transcends or goes beyond the social. Similarly, religion goes beyond or transcends culture to the extent that a religion orients human beings into the Divine Mystery, which transcends all cultural achievements and grounds all truth, goodness, and holiness. To the extent that a religion or a culture fails in this transcendent orientation to the Divine, they fall into forms of what prophets denounced as idolatry. That which one worships and prays to religiously should not be one's ideas or images or constructs of the Divine, but the Divine as Divine. The transcendence of the cultural over the social rests, as Christopher Dawson saw, upon the genuinely religious:

> We are only just beginning to understand how intimately and profoundly the vitality of a society is bound up with its religion. It is the religious impulse which supplies the cohesive force which unifies a society and a culture. The great civilizations of the world do not produce the great religions as a kind of cultural by-product; in a very real sense, the great religions are the foundations on which the great civilizations rest. A society which has lost its religion becomes sooner or later a society which has lost its culture.[6]

The recent collapse of communist cultures in Eastern Europe and the former Soviet Union might provide illustrations of this relation of religion to culture.

While sharing in this general transcendence of the religious over the cultural, the Gospel makes far more specifically transcendent claims. The Gospel transcends or goes beyond the cultural even more radically than the cultural goes beyond the social. For the Gospel is not the practice or product of human creativity, nor of the human orientation toward the Divine; rather, the Gospel is constituted by the missions of the Word and the Spirit to redeem humankind. As with culture, so with the Gospel, it is important to distinguish between the faith by which the believer learns and knows the truth of the Gospel, and what the believer knows. This is the distinction of *fides qua* and *fides quae*—the light of faith and the affirmations of faith. It is crucial that this distinction not be misread in a typically Cartesian framework whereby believing is as subjective as thinking and what is believed are only ideas or propositions. Just as the light of faith is not a human achievement but a gift from God, so the dynamism of the act of faith is not toward

---

6 Christopher Dawson, *Enquiries into Religion and Culture* (London: Sheed & Ward, 1937), 115.

propositions but, through the affirmations of faith to God, as God is in God-self. Because the Church knows God as God is through the light of faith, she is able to express this knowledge of reality in the creeds and doctrines of faith.

In this faith is similar to other forms of human knowledge, for it is only on the basis of knowing realities that the human mind expresses that knowledge in propositions and statements. As Thomas Aquinas remarks:

> Actus enim credentis non terminatur ad enuntiabile, sed ad rem: non enim formamus enuntiabilia nisi ut per ea de rebus cognitionem habeamus, sicut in scientia, ita et in fide. (*Summa theologiae* II–II, q. 1, a. 2, ad 2)

Knowing is very different from thinking, and faith is a form of knowing.

Within any culture there is present, insofar as any culture is consti-tuted by human minds and human actions, both a transcendental and an immanent dimension. Any genuine culture is both transcultural and incultural. It is transcultural insofar as it fosters the beauty of the aesthetic, the truth of intelligence, the goodness of morality, the holiness of the reli-gious. These transcultural dimensions are not merely "ideals" or "ideas" reserved in some eternal thought: They are *trans*cultural orientations that are always inculturated in particular achievements of beautiful art, achievements of genial intelligence, achievements of moral goodness, achievements of religious holiness.[7] While cultural achievements are always limited and concretely situated, the transcultural orientations of the human spirit assure that limitations and the radical pluralism of cul-tural situations do not justify historicism and total cultural relativism. If cultural anthropology witnesses to anything, it is the concrete capacities for intercultural communication and exchange. Multiculturalism would be impossible if all cultures were incommensurable and completely other.

The tension between the transcultural and the incultural is, of course, heightened radically by the revelation of the covenants of God with Israel and the Incarnation of the Word in the new covenant of redemption in the life, death, and resurrection of Jesus Christ. The absolutely supernatural

---

[7] Cf. Hans Urs von Balthasar, *Theological Anthropology* (New York: Sheed & Ward, 1967); K. Rahner, SJ, *Theological Investigations*, vol. XVI, trans. David Morland (New York: Crossroad, 1983), 3–34, 60–78; idem, *Foundations of Christian Faith*, trans. William Dych (New York: Crossroad, 1978), 24–89; Matthew Lamb, "The Notion of the Transcultural in Lonergan," *Method: Journal of Lonergan Studies*, 9(2).

gift of the Triune God's redemptive love in the missions of the Word and Spirit embrace the totality of human history with all of its multiple cultures. The absolute transcendence of the Triune God should not be, as it too often is, imaginatively projected as if it was not also the absolute immanence of God who is more intimate to all creatures than they are to themselves. So the gift of redemption is in basic harmony, as St. Athanasius put it so well, with the symphonic gift of creation. As absolute transcendence and totally free gift is in no way antithetical to, but indeed grounds, the absolute immanence of God's gifted presence; as the eternal procession of the Word from the Father is in no way antithetical to, but actually brings about, the incarnation of the Word in the womb of the Virgin Mary; so the transcultural dimension of the Gospel is in no way antithetical to, but makes really possible, the inculturation of the Gospel in myriad cultures. Because the Gospel is absolutely supernatural and totally the free gift of an all-loving Triune God, the Gospel must be proclaimed and inculturated among all nations and cultures.

Catholic Theological Resources for Inculturation

It is very important to understand the transcultural dimension of the Gospel correctly in order to avoid the mistake of imagining that the process of inculturation was somehow one of distilling some "essence" or *"kurzformel"* of the Gospel—as if the "essence" were transhistorical or transtemporal and could then be planted like a flag on the shores of any random culture. There is no essence or short formula of the Gospel that renders it transcultural. Rather it is the Person of Jesus Christ, the Word Incarnate, who, with the Father and the Spirit, is the Lord of history and whose Infinite Understanding, Knowing, and Loving brings everything into being—including all the human minds, hearts, and hands that create the myriad cultures in human history.

The interpersonal immediacy and presence of the Triune God is not one that negates mediations, rather the Triune Presence creates all the mediations. Our Catholic faith, as both the Greek and Latin theologians reminds us, commits us to the whole, the καθ᾽ ὅλον, of God's revelatory presence. The orthodox center never succumbed to the Gnostic temptation to set the Divine Spiritual Presence and Immediacy in opposition to the historical mediations. For us in the West, this affirmation of the Divine immediacy mediated concretely and communally through the Israel, the Incarnation, and the ongoing mission of the Church in her sacraments and ministries was most emphatically narrated in St. Augustine's theology. Any effort to reject historical mediations in the name of a purely spiritual immediacy was condemned as a rejection of the Word Incarnate and his Spirit. Pure Infinite Intelligence, Love, and Act created all that is, and it was only among intellectual creatures, who shared in what is most divine in all creation, that sin and evil could enter through a prideful blindness to the mediation of beauty, truth, goodness, and holiness.

It is in and through the sacramental communion of the Church that the mission of the Word and the Spirit finds historical mediation. The sacramental mediation clearly continues the divine-human interpersonal communion, and it emphasizes how symbol and ritual practice mediates sacred realities. One finds within the sacraments precisely the ongoing dynamism of the transcultural realities of Christ in Glory and the Communion of Saints inculturated in myriad different cultures and peoples. As sacramental the transcultural catholicity or universality of the Church is not an abstract idea or essence, rather it is a concrete universality that is realized in and through inculturation within local communities that, through the sacramental mediation of their episcopal pastors, are in communion with the local Church of Rome, and its bishop, the pope, who is charged in a very special way with the ministry of unity.

The sacramental mediation of the Immediacy of the Triune God is particularly difficult to grasp and practice in a post-Enlightenment culture that has lost institutional mediations of the quest for wisdom as a true concern for, and contemplation of, the whole. The eclipse of wisdom—Nietzsche's Zarathustra is "weary of wisdom"—leads to the fragmentation of unity and the loss of any sense of authority as genuine service of the truth. With the loss of wisdom traditions, modern cultures cultivate empirical sciences of the particular. There is no heuristic attention to the intelligibility and pattern of the whole; instead there is attention only to the individual things, and any effort to pattern or order them are taken to be conventional. The encyclopedists attend carefully to the endless particularities open to human study, but lack any internal intelligent ordering of the whole. The alphabet provides the bureaucrats with their impoverished substitute for order: the filing system. The genealogists then come along to claim that any language is only a dialect with an army and a navy, so that all orders are only systems of dominative power. Truth becomes just another name for power.[8]

---

8 Cf. A. MacIntyre, *Three Rival Versions of Moral Enquiry* (Notre Dame, IN: University of Notre Dame Press, 1990).

In this context there is no possibility of discerning the vast difference between authority and authoritarianism. Power is not attributed to wisdom and truth, but is seen as only arbitrary decisions dominatively imposing the "ideas" of the ruling class. Institutions are not defined as patterns of cooperation but rather, as in Max Weber, as structures of domination *(Herrschaftsstrukturen)*. As Weber cynically remarks, the only difference between hereditary and democratic institutions is that in the latter the subjects get to elect who will dominate them. Since all institutions in this context are more or less dominative, it is only by being completely autonomous in one's monadic individuality that one has full freedom. This then reduces the church to no more than just another "voluntary associations of like-minded believers"—and the fragmentation of Christian churches makes them hardly more than clubs in a post-Enlightenment culture. Not only is ecclesial unity as patterns of cooperative communion threatened, along with any effective authority dedicated to preserving the unity of faith, but the constitutive and effective functions of the ecclesial symbols are diminished as all symbols are reduced to merely conventional signs that are left up to the consensus of like-minded congregations.

In such a culture the transformative task of the Catholic Church is to maintain its sacramental mediation, and this means preserving intact the episcopal communion in the ongoing preaching, teaching, and liturgical practice of the faith. We are used to reading the emphasis in Vatican II on episcopal collegiality as a complement to Vatican I's emphasis on papal authority. Collegial authority, however, can also be read as a much needed critical corrective to the privatization of Christianity in modern cultures, along with the loss of episcopal ministry as one of communion and the teaching of the wisdom of the faith. Among the many resources in our Catholic heritage that are needed today, I doubt that any other institution has such a vast and differentiated literature on the proper and wise discernment by and of authority and its many functions in the Church. This is to a large extent an untapped resource in our time, but one that is very needed in our time.

Theologians have very special responsibilities in making available the resources within Catholic traditions for the tasks of inculturation. The theological task is daunting because of the immense labors of learning required in appropriating almost two millennia of theological reflection in so many varied cultural contexts. Multiculturalism is not simply synchronic, addressing only those cultures now existing, but also diachronic, attentive to the cultures of the past. Fundamental to a Catholic orientation in this is also to insist that

cultural differences are not always differences that are contradictory. Difference or otherness is not to be placed in a framework of opposition and in a
struggle for supremacy. Differences can be complementary: Different cultures
manifesting the wealth of the human spirit so that one culture brings out vir-
tualities or capacities that, while different from those emergent in others, still
complement them. Many criticisms of Eurocentrism, for example, are cast in
terms of power and domination, but ignore the very important complementary aspects of cultures in Europe and the abiding importance of the contributions to human living made by European cultures. Differences can also be
genetic when one culture actualizes capacities that emerge from the achievements of other cultures and presupposes them (e.g., urban cultures are possible only by presupposing and depending upon agrarian cultures).

   Cultural differences are contradictory only when one culture affirms
the same realities that another culture denies. Such a dialectic of contradictory cultural differences calls for explicit attention to the transcultural
foundations of culture both (1) in human mind as *imago Dei* constituting
and effecting cultures; and (2) in the revelation of God in Christ Jesus. For
it is only with such attention that transcultural norms can be found with
which to judge the contradictory claims of the differing cultures.

   The tasks of inculturation involve discerning such complementary,
genetic, and dialectical differences in the process of learning the cultures
while evangelizing them. In Catholic theological traditions we have much
that can aid our contemporary responsibilities. Theology is an ongoing
learning process whereby the Church comes to understand in ever more
diverse ways the Mysteries revealed in our faith in the Word Incarnate. There
is an ongoing discovery of the human mind and creation inspired by the
quest for understanding the Gospel. Faith, as a knowledge engendered by the
Spirit of Love poured forth in our hearts (Rom 5:5), is a movement from the
Triune God above downward from Love, and the truth or knowledge born
of love, to understanding and the communication of the faith in words and
deeds. The movement of faith from above downward, so to speak, in no way
inhibits—but rather fosters—a movement of the human mind from below
upward, from experiencing the words and deeds of faith through efforts to
understand them correctly, to the threshold of responsible decision and love.
When we say that theology is constituted by faith and reason, what is
implied is precisely this twofold movement of faith and reason.[9]

_____

   [9] For example, von Balthasar's *pistis* and *gnosis* in *The Glory of the Lord*, vol. 1 (San Fran-
      cisco: Ignatius Press, 1982), 131ff.; Rahner's mystery and question in *Foundations of*

In Catholic theology the higher does not negate in any way the lower: So the Infinite does not negate but creates the finite, Spiritual does not negate but creates the material, the Eternal does not negate but creates the temporal, and so on. So the movement from above downward, from God to creation, in no way denigrates but makes possible the movement from below upward. It is, in my judgment, a failure to appreciate this that has led so many modern theologians to imagine an opposition, for example, between a "Christology from Above" and a "Christology from below." In fact, given the violence and massive injustice throughout human history, any sober and realistic assessment would lead us to realize how only the highest Christology would be able to bring good out of evil, life out of death, grace out of sin, the kingdom of God and perfect justice out of the injustice and death of this life.

Another corollary that follows from this is that the incomprehensibility of God is not to predicate some absolute unknowability of the Divine Being. Indeed, Thomas Aquinas clearly differentiates the incomprehensibility of God from any claim of "unknowability." We shall never, even in glory, exhaustively understand the Triune God, but we shall know God as God is. The knowledge born of supernatural love that faith is, is indeed a knowledge. Even without faith, we can know that God is. The difference between incomprehensibility and unknowability is the difference between understanding and judgment. In faith we *know* the revealed Divine mysteries such as the Trinity and the Incarnation of the Word. These truths are known in the judgment and assent of faith. Those judgments, through the light of faith, mediate a true knowledge of the Divine Realities. While these are incomprehensible to our finite reason, they are not thereby unknown any more than we would say that the Triune God was "unlovable." As St. Augustine very astutely remarks, we never love the unknown, rather we love to know the unknown. Thus those theologians who argue from the unknowability of God to a claim either that the great Trinitarian or Christological councils were only "inculturating" faith in Jesus in a Greek milieu, or that we can leave those dogmas behind as we inculturate the Gospel in other cultures, are simply ignoring the most basic intentionality of both our reason and the Catholic faith itself.

The twofold movement in theology underlies a fourfold set of differentiations constituting the theological wisdom traditions. The differentiations

---

Christian Faith, 44–89; Lonergan's notion of faith as a knowledge born of love and the two phases of functional specialization in *Method of Theology* (New York: Herder & Herder, 1972), 101–45.

are those (1) between Scripture and (2) doctrines; between doctrines and (3) systematics; and finally between systematics and (4) historicity. Historically later differentiations in Catholic theology in no way negate or lessen earlier developments. Karl Rahner radically revised the notion of "Aufhebung" or "sublation" from that so central to Hegel's philosophy of history. Sublation preserves and elevates but does not involve, as it does for Hegel, negation. From the condemnations of Marcionism to the criticisms of Modernism, Catholic teaching refuses to pit the new against the old, as if it would negate or completely replace the old. This is especially important in a post-Enlightenment culture such as ours in the United States, where the new tends to be cast as a negation of the old, where innovation is opposed to tradition.

While contemporary theologians readily acknowledge the differentiations of Scripture, and usually see the centrality of historicity or historical consciousness for the modern period, the doctrinal and systematic differentiations are usually ignored. Often one finds among these theologians a tendency to treat the differentiation of doctrine from Scripture as no more than an "inculturation" of the Gospel message in what for us today is a very foreign "Greek world" (so the all too frequent identifications of this differentiation as "Hellenization"). The arguments of Aloys Grillmeier, Bernard Lonergan, and John Courtney Murray against the historicist reduction of the "Hellenization thesis" are not adequately understood today. As Murray remarked: Hellenization is a "learned absurdity." Indeed, one wonders how St. Athanasius would view such efforts, given his treatise "Against the Greeks" and his expulsions from his diocese, as he sought refuge among the nuns and monks of the dessert.[10]

To understand the differentiation of doctrine from Scripture in the great Trinitarian and Christological councils it is important to attend to the central concern for conversion and the intellectual-spiritual praxis of discipleship after the age of the martyrs. The early Christians had in the preaching and praxis of the Apostles and martyrs the clear transcultural witness to the Lord of all cultures. The law of the cross, as lived out in the witness of martyrdom, manifests the transformative suffering intrinsic to the inculturation of the Gospel in any culture. When the age of persecution ended, this transforma-

---

10 Cf. Aloys Grillmeier, *Christ in the Christian Tradition*, vol. 1, trans. John Bowden (Atlanta: John Knox Press, 1975), 249–73, 308–28; Bernard Lonergan, SJ, "The Dehellenization of Dogma," in *Second Collection* (Philadelphia: Westminster Press, 1974), 11–32; John Courtney Murray, SJ, *The Problem of God* (New Haven, CT: Yale University Press, 1964), 31–60. Also Douglas Burton-Christie, *Word in the Desert* (Oxford: Oxford University Press, 1993).

tive and eschatological witness of discipleship was carried forward, not only
in the worship of the Church, but also in the monastic and religious life.

What was at stake was precisely the transcendence of the Triune God
and redemption in Christ, so that a false "inculturation" was avoided,
which would have made the Christian faith into a legitimation of the
Roman Empire.[11] The doctrinal differentiation has to do with the cultivation of the intellectual dimensions of the Gospel faith. Far from "Hellenizing" the Gospel, the doctrines proclaim and protect the realities revealed
in the Gospel by insisting upon the truth of the judgments of faith-
enlightened reason. There is, as Lonergan analyzes, an ongoing discovery
of mind in the development of doctrines.[12] As St. Anthony remarked in
his fourth letter, Arius was led into error because he did not attend to his
own mind *(nous)* as enlightened by the Word of God.[13] The entire religious ascesis aimed at humility and purity of heart was to enable Christians to so refine and reorient their experience so that they could attend
experientially to the truth and wisdom revealed in Christ Jesus.

The importance of this orthopraxis nurturing orthodoxy had enormous
importance for inculturating the Gospel throughout both East and West.[14]
The Gospel was to be spread by genuine discipleship, not by the sword and
dominative power. Recall the thousands of monastic communities of
women and men who lived among the "barbarians" and brought them to
Christ. Far from being like evangelistic sects, the monasteries embodied the
contemplative and intellectual dimensions of genuine Catholic faith, integrating native cultures while also preserving the great classical patrimony of
Greece and Rome.[15] There is no substitution for genuine discipleship of the
crucified and risen Lord in the tasks of inculturation.

The differentiation of doctrine emphasized the wisdom of the Truth
of faith, and how the judgment of faith is not an arbitrary decision of the
will but an assent informed with the light of faith healing and intensifying
the light of reason. The realities revealed in the Sacred Scriptures, as they

---

[11] Cf. E. Peterson, "Monotheismus als politisches Problem," in his *Theologische Trak-
tate* (Munich: Kösel Verlag, 1951).

[12] Cf. Bernard Lonergan, *Method in Theology* (Toronto: University of Toronto Press),
305–20.

[13] Cf. Samuel Rubenson, *The Letters of St. Anthony,* trans. Derwas J. Chitty (Oxford:
SLG Press, 1991), 9–13.

[14] Cf. Hans Urs von Balthasar, *Explorations in Theology,* vol. II (San Francisco: Ignatius
Press, 1991), 333ff.

[15] Cf. C. Dawson, *The Making of Europe* (New York: Sheed & Ward, 1945), 189–290.

are read and prayed within the worshiping Christian community, led not only to the doctrinal differentiation but to the systematic as well. The quest for understanding took on an explicitly metaphysical set of terms and relations in the flowering of systematic theology as the universities emerged from the monastic and cathedral schools.

Theology is both a wisdom and a "science." The differentiation called for a rather rigorous intellectual development. Terms such as grace, sacrament, nature, form, matter, *esse,* and the like, which were used in a more globally compact and descriptive manner, now took on definitions that required an intellectual conversion capable of clearly differentiating the mind from the physical and imaginative. This differentiation was most important in the task of inculturating the Gospel within the emerging university cultures. As the monasteries had institutionalized, in the sense of set-up patterns of living, the quest for wisdom and holiness, so now the new universities would institutionalize the quest for science.

As with any process of differentiation, there is the danger of a failure of appropriation. Cut off from the appropriative exercises of a love-informed faith and wisdom, the scriptural differentiation can be distorted into a mere literalism or fundamentalism; the doctrinal can be distorted into a propositionalism and authoritarian dogmatism. So the systematic differentiation, severed from a living wisdom, can be distorted into an arrogant and arid conceptualism. When this occurred in theology, the stage was set for the rather massive severance of wisdom from science that is so evident in today's universities and cultures.

Too few of those who came after Aquinas realized, as he did, that the subject of the science of theology is neither faith nor religious experience but God. Just as there can be no genuine inculturation of the Gospel except in the presence of the transcultural Word Incarnate, so there can be no genuine inculturation of wisdom in a university culture except in the realization of how all intellectual excellence is but a faint image of Infinite Wisdom generating Infinite Truth spirating Infinite Love. When that realization was lost, so was any unifying wisdom, and universities became multiversities, as the ordering functions of wisdom were farmed out to logicians and nominalists.

Rejecting the subsequent differentiations of doctrine and systematics, the Reformers sought a return to the Scriptures alone. As the unifying role of wisdom was lost in the universities, so the unifying function of ecclesial ministry was lost. The ensuing wars of religion left the public realm open to the secularists as the intellectual realm became the preserve of encyclo-pedists and genealogists.

The differentiation of historicity from systematics is as problematic as it is for Catholic theology precisely because there is such a strong tendency to skip from our modern historical situation back to the scriptural differ-entiations without any, or only the most superficial, acquaintance with doctrinal and systematic differentiations. Ironically, in the name of history and historical consciousness extremely important achievements of Catholic doctrine and theology are ignored or relegated to past inculturations that have little or no interest for us today. Unfortunately, not a single history of Catholic theology has been written by Catholic theologians in North America in the past three decades. The histories used in most Catholic graduate courses, when not by European Catholics, have been Protestant histories that understandably had very different evaluations of the doctri-nal and systematic differentiations. Little wonder, then, that one finds hardly any difference between those whose graduate studies are done in Catholic doctoral programs and those done in the major Protestant Divin-ity Schools.

Indeed, doctrinal and systematic theology is very much the stepchild of modern academic theology. There are societies and journals devoted exclu-sively to Biblical, Historical, and Moral theology. There is not one society or journal anywhere devoted exclusively to doctrinal and systematic theology. Without measuring up to the scriptural, doctrinal, and systematic achieve-ments of the past, contemporary theologians are prey to collapsing historic-ity into a very ahistorical historism. Historicism is in fact the offspring of nominalism; all that we have from history, so historicism contends, are the external words, documents, monuments—whatever the data of sense pres-ent to us. The constitutive meanings and normative values that can discern historical progress from decline, genuineness from alienation, are lost. Mind is not minded. So historicism in the university mirrors the general malaise of a sensate and consumerist culture. Catholic theology has important resources to heal and transform such academic and cultural situations. But to bring those resources to bear upon the problems requires that the differ-entiations of historical consciousness measure up to the achievements of the scriptural, doctrinal, and systematic.

Without these previous differentiations clear in the minds of Catholic theologians, they do not really understand the development of doctrine and the development of systematic understandings of those doctrines and how they promote a graced understanding. What they do not understand they tend to reject or belittle or set aside. So we have the call for "Biblical Pre-Nicean" Christologies or Trinitarian theologies. This is to deny and reject what is constitutive of our theological traditions. It is a retrograde effort at de-differentiation, at claiming that we need not bother learning the doctrinal or systematic differentiations since they were either "defeated" or "wrong-headed." So also we have Catholic theologians who simply cannot tell the difference between the doctrinal differentiations and a process of Hellenizing the Christian faith.

All this eventually will pose rather grave pastoral problems. The bishops simply cannot allow the very heart of our Trinitarian and Christological faith—the Person of Our Lord Jesus Christ and his Father and the Holy Spirit—to be emptied into symbols and concepts for the recondite reflections of disaffected theologians. Sooner rather than later pastoral practice will be adversely impacted. In taking action a bishop might be passed off as being "authoritarian" to the degree that the development of the differentiations are very rare within the Catholic theological community. Recall St. Athanasius finding almost the whole world Arian.

Concluding Questions: American Culture and Catholic Transformation

By way of conclusion, allow me to pose some issues regarding the inculturation of the Gospel in the United States. For the sake of discussion, I will state them in rather stark terms.

First, the United States of America is the only fully post-Enlightenment culture in the entire world. With the exception of the Native Americans, the U.S. has no indigenous population whose collective memory predates the Enlightenment. Immigration was to a *novus ordo saeculorum* so that both conservatives and progressives would politically appeal to a very liberal set of documents—the Declaration of Independence and the Constitution. In light of this, is not Catholicism, as a transnational and transcultural and multiethnic *institutionalized* religion, with a unity mediated through apostolic succession of pope and bishops, in a very peculiar stance vis-à-vis American culture? Protestantism, with its national ecclesial structures, has had a far more formative influence upon the founding experiences and history of the United States than Catholicism. Are we not perhaps now in a position to appreciate how the "foreign" character of Catholicism was not so much a result of the ethnic immigrants as it is of the unresolved dialectic between Catholicism and the Enlightenment, Catholicism and modernism? The remaining issues spell out some of this dialectic.

Second, there are three fundamental stances that run throughout all major Enlightenment thinkers (conservative, liberal, radical) with which Catholicism (along with Judaism) cannot agree. The first is that reality is ultimately conflictual (Machiavelli, Hobbes, Locke, Hume, Marx); the second is that knowledge is power, discovering laws in order to impose conventional order upon monadized phenomena (Hobbes, Bacon, Leibniz, Franklin, Freud); and the third is the social correlative of the first two, namely, that social and cultural institutions are structures of legitimate domination whereby monadic individuals more or less agree to the forms of legitimate coercion (legal force and fear) required to establish and maintain the conventional orders of enlightened society (Hobbes, Hume, Smith, Marx, Weber). Within this context, freedom is freedom to pursue one's own individual self-interest. Freedom is basically value-neutral, for any supra-individual norm is taken as no more than conventional, and so imposed either by dictate or by consensus. There are only, then, procedural norms—no substantiative norms—for what is good. Hence the distinction between legality and morality is a distinction without a difference. In a word, there is the instrumentalization of nature, life, and society.

Does not Catholicism offer a very different orientation? Reality is not ultimately conflictual but rather the result of an all good God creating the universe in, to use Athanasius's imagery, symphonic harmony. Dissonance or conflict arise only from the sin of intelligent creatures, and then God restores the beauty by redemption. Knowledge is not power but the understanding of the truth. Wisdom orders all things, including the exercise of power, not vice versa. Faith is a knowledge born of love, not a knowledge born of fear or force. In God's infinite wisdom he chose to remove evil, not through Divine power, but by transforming evil into good through the sufferings of his only Son on the Cross.

Institutions are primarily patterns of cooperation through which the common good is known and effected. There is no prepolitical state of nature in which we have isolated monadic individuals; rather human beings are naturally social and political. Freedom, therefore, is not value-neutral but oriented toward the truly good. Freedom intrinsically, by our very created natures, finds its norm in the truly good. As long as our desires are properly ordered, as we choose the good, our freedom expands.

Insofar as our desires are disordered, and we choose evil, our freedom contracts. Law is not instrumental, aimed at imposing arbitrary orders, but is fundamentally educative in the good.

Third, two of the key institutions of the Enlightenment were the schools and the hospitals. Education and health care are taken to be fundamental to "life, liberty, and the pursuit of happiness." Now, within the United States Catholics have built up the largest non-public educational system and the largest non-public health care system in world history. The ideals of enlightenment through education and just care for the weak and ill transcend the cultural or philosophical frameworks mentioned above. I would want to argue that any effective transformative presence of Catholicism within American culture will demand that we strengthen these educational and health-care institutions in their distinctively Catholic identity. This requires special attention now since those institutions are no longer being carried by a predominantly religious or clerical faculty or staff. Central will be the religious, moral, and intellectual formation of laypeople and religious alike.

Fourth, to foster this formation the universities and seminaries are crucial. Serious inculturation will demand that we overcome the cultural deficiencies of post-Enlightenment culture. While the empiricism and positivism of the first Enlightenment may still dominate, Lonergan traces the emergence of what he terms a second enlightenment that, from its cultural origins in the relativizing of Euclidean geometry, relativity theories, and quantum mechanics, has moved on to challenge empiricism and positivism in economics, politics, and the deductivist pretensions of both empiricism and idealism in philosophy.

> Of itself this second enlightenment is culturally significant. But it may have as well a social mission. Just as the first enlightenment had its carrier in the transition from feudal to bourgeois society, so the second may find a role and task in offering hope and providing leadership to the masses alienated by large establishments under bureaucratic management.[16]

Formation in the intellectual, moral, and theological virtues would go a long way in providing the leadership required to overcome the alienation so widespread in a culture that is attempting bureaucratic and instrumen-

---

16 Bernard Lonergan, *A Third Collection* (New York: Paulist Press, 1985), 63–65.

talist control by passing ever more rules and laws. Such a second enlightenment is just what is needed if we are to address the ravages of monadic individualism, with its ever-increasing nihilism. Democracy is intellectually, morally, and religiously good *only to the extent* that its citizens are well educated, virtuous, and holy. Any attempt to skirt this demand for virtuous citizens by pretending that all a democracy needs is the consent of the governed to the laws and constitutions of the land is belied by the daily experience of crime, violence, and socio-cultural disintegration. There simply is no substitute for virtue—however much democracy was thought to be such. No significant truth or goodness is assured by only stressing one person, one vote—for then the votes of the fool and the criminal are just as "significant" as the votes of the wise and the good.

Finally, given sin and the massive injustices in human history, the importance of holiness and the theological virtues cannot be overestimated in the tasks of inculturation. The fact that theology has disappeared from the cultural patrimony of our post-Enlightenment intellectual establishment has meant that empirical science is bereft of the wisdom it so desperately needs. The empirical sciences are charting how human beings behave, how they act. They are ascribing that behavior—no matter how violent and sinful it is—to human nature. On the basis of such studies social policies are formulated, and so the violence and sin become structured into the society and culture. In such cycles of social and cultural decline the intellectually virtuous tend toward cynicism, while the morally virtuous tend toward stoicism.

The intelligent quest for wisdom and science, as well as the moral quest for justice, cannot succumb to cynicism and indifference. Because our kingdom is not of this world, we can dedicate ourselves to the creative and redemptive transformation of this world. Because through faith, hope, and love we are in communion with the absolutely transcendent Triune God, we are members of one another in the historically immanent mediations of the missions of the Word and the Spirit to bring about the kingdom of God in our time and culture.

Catholicism in America is at a decisive *kairos*, for the negative aspects of our post-Enlightenment culture are becoming ever more manifest. Will we Catholics contribute significantly to building up a more intelligent, good, and just culture—a civilization and culture of love to which John Paul II exhorts us? Or will we succumb to the distractions and illusions of the culture of death? Ironically, modernity and the Enlightenment rejected the supposed "other-worldly" longing of Christianity for the kingdom of God in eternal life. The new culture would dedicate human beings totally to "this-worldly" efforts in the tasks of economic and technological progress. Now we find that by this truncation of human consciousness to "this-world"—cut off from its creative and redemptive enfolding in the Reality of the Triune God—we become disgusted with this life to such an extent that many see nothing wrong with practices of death such as abortion and euthanasia. Obviously, we cannot genuinely love this world without a strong longing for the perfection of this world in the world to come.

7

Communicative Praxis and Theology: Beyond Modern Nihilism and Dogmatism

> *Die große Scholastik, vorab die Summen des Thomas,*
> *hatten ihre Kraft und Würde daran, daß sie, ohne den*
> *Begriff der Vernunft zu verabsolutieren, nirgends ihn*
> *verfemten: dazu ging die Theologie erst im Zeitalter*
> *des Nominalismus, zumal bei Luther, über.*
>
> —Theodor W. Adorno
> *Vernunft und Offenbarung* (1957)

THE RELEVANCE of the critical theory for a theology of the public realm is, perhaps, a suitable occasion to peer beneath the surfaces of critical theory, rummage under the stage of its splendid (if often frustrating) conceptuality, and encounter the deformed dwarf of theology, described by Walter Benjamin as an underground agent in philosophical discourse. In his own way, Benjamin applied to dialectical philosophers what Nietzsche said of German philosophers: *"Was sind sie, dann, wenn nicht hinterlistige Theologen?"*[1]

This essay was originally published as "Communicative Praxis and Theology: Beyond Modern Nihilism and Dogmatism" in Don S. Browning and Francis S. Fiorenza, eds. *Habermas, Modernity, and Public Theology* (New York: Crossroad, 1992), 92–118. Just before his election as pope, Cardinal Ratzinger dialogued with Jürgen Habermas, see their *The Dialectics of Secularization: On Reason and Religion* (San Francisco: Ignatius Press, 2006).

[1] Walter Benjamin, *Zur Kritik der Gewalt und andere Aufsätze* (Frankfurt: Suhrkamp, 1965), 78. Theodor Adorno's essay "Vernunft und Offenbarung" can be found in *Stichworte: Kritische Modelle 2* (Frankfurt: Suhrkamp, 1969), 20–28.

Has not the jargon of authenticity given way to a jargon of publicity? Is not sophism alive and well in the great communication networks of our age? Are not all forms of communication in danger of being reduced to utilitarian and pragmatic "communicative techniques"? Could it be that modernity provides the best communication networks in world history, but has nothing substantive to communicate? Is not informed political participation waning precisely in those cultures with omnipresent television? Are not individuals in those cultures less empowered to engage in understanding their own narratives and more to adopt the packaged narratives of talk shows and soap operas? Are we really communicating in this age of instantaneous communication?

Immanuel Kant defined the Enlightenment as emerging out of immaturity by having the courage to use publicly one's own understanding. We now, as Johann Baptist Metz recently wrote, have a crisis of a second-order immaturity in which the public forum of "enlightened" societies fails to support vigorous and reasoned public debate and consequently political participation declines. Politics and communication have been so instrumentalized that serious judgments are rarely made and even more rarely communicated.[2]

Philosophers of communication and culture in the age of communications are not unlike theologians in the age of faith. Dialectical discernment is imperative. The traditions of critical theory teach important lessons in dialectical discernment in how they criticize the instrumentalism and functionalism and yet avoid romanticism and historicism.

I will argue here that theology can contribute creatively and transformatively to an understanding of communicative praxis that avoids the nihilism and dogmatism threatening modernist and postmodernist discourses. First, I will sketch a few of the lines that link modern dogmatism and nihilism, suggesting that the dogmatic self-assertion of modernity evokes its shadow, nihilism. Then I will argue that what is normative in modernity is communicative praxis understood as a process of raising ever further relevant questions. Finally, I will suggest three areas in which communicative praxis and theology help to realize reason in history and to remove those distortions that cast religion in utilitarian or fanatical roles.

---

2 Immanuel Kant, "Beantwortung der Frage: Was ist Aufklärung?" *Werke XI* (Frankfurt: Suhrkamp, 1964), 53–61; Johann B. Metz "Wider die zweite Unmündigkeit" in *Frankfurter Allgemeine Zeitung*, 15 December 1987.

Modern Nihilism and Dogmatism

Modernity Is Now History

Modernity is no longer modern.[3] Modernity now has to be defended in the name of continuity, moderation, even tradition.[4] It may be that the postmodernists are no more than ultramodernists, but they hardly exemplify modern rational self-assurance. The defenders of the modern project, the *via moderna*, now adopt an orientation that the defenders of the *viae antiquae* (ancient, medieval, and renaissance) used before them. The modern way is not only self-critical, we are told, but its central orientation is toward mutual understanding rather than coercive domination. Reading Jürgen Habermas's brilliant and incisive *The Philosophical Discourse of Modernity*, I was reminded of Friedrich Schleiermacher's *On Religion: Speeches to its Cultured Despisers*. What modernity once did unto religion in the name of a supposedly pure reason, is now done unto modern reason—its purity long tarnished if not extinguished.[5]

"Self-critical," "mutual understanding," and "reciprocal recognition" are hardly hallmarks of modern history; any more than the moral and intellectual virtues were hallmarks of ancient Greece or Rome; the theological virtues of faith, hope, and love were hallmarks of medieval history; or absolute faith in Christ's Gospel was a hallmark of the Reformation. Modernity now has a history and discrete repentance should be the order of the day. The name of discretion is ambiguity. Analogous to the orientation David Tracy takes to religion in *Plurality and Ambiguity*, Habermas calls attention to the ambiguity intrinsic to modern processes of rationalization.[6]

Hans Blumenberg's arguments for the legitimacy of modernity cut both ways. The autonomy of modernity means that it is intrinsically responsible

---

[3] Jean-François Lyotard, *The Postmodern Condition: A Report on Knowledge,* trans. G. Bennington and B. Massumi (Minneapolis: University of Minnesota Press, 1984) and *Le Différend* (Paris: Editions de Minuit, 1983).

[4] Cf. David Kolb, *The Critique of Pure Modernity: Hegel, Heidegger and After* (Chicago: The University of Chicago Press, 1986), 256ff.

[5] Cf. Jürgen Habermas, *The Philosophical Discourse of Modernity,* trans. Frederick Lawrence (Cambridge, MA: MIT Press, 1987). On parallels from the past, see Richard Jones, *Ancients and Moderns: A Study of the Rise of the Scientific Movement in Seventeenth-Century England.* (St. Louis, MO: Washington University Press, 1961); Emile Poulat, *Modernistica: Horizons, Physionomies, Débats* (Paris: Nouvelles Éditions Latines, 1982); Lucien Febvre, *The Problem of Unbelief in the Sixteenth Century: The Religion of Rabelais,* trans. B. Gottlieb (Cambridge, MA: Harvard University Press, 1982), 335–464.

[6] Ibid., xv.

for its own horrors. The easy ascription of these horrors to mythic or pre-modern residues illustrates, in my judgment, reasons degenerating into rationalizations.[7] The defenders of modernity keep insisting on what they think are its undeniable achievements. The cultured despisers of modernity concentrate on its palpable distortions. Today belief in automatic progress through science and technology is intellectually and morally indefensible, and modernity needs self-reassurance *(Selbstvergewisserung)* that escapes the cycle of dogmatic self-assertion countering nihilistic condemnation.

Those who critically defend modernity must recognize that dogmatic self-assertion resides at the heart of the modern age. Hans-Georg Gadamer's critique of the Enlightenment's *Vorurteil gegen Vorurteile*, Wayne Booth's critique of the modern dogmas of scientism and motivism, and Alasdair Mac-Intyre's critiques of emotive individualism and liberalism do more than suggest that enlightened modernity is reaping the harsh value-judgments it has sown against other periods and cultures.[8] How enlightened and true were the judgments forcing previous generations into prehistories of modern developments?

Third- and fourth-world critics who want to do to modernity what modernity did to the Middle Ages and Renaissance are more strident: They use modernity's tools (science and technology) but negate its culture.[9] These harsher critiques haunt first- and second-world debates as the limits to industrial growth and mounting global pollution pose the question: Are massive poverty and misery in the third and fourth worlds remnants of modernity's past that progress will eventually eradicate, or intimations of our fated future? Are we left with the choice but to join

---

7 Hans Blumenberg, *The Legitimacy of Modernity,* trans. Robert Wallace (Cambridge: MIT Press, 1984). For readings of modernity that expose the horror, see Zygmunt Bauman, *Modernity and the Holocaust* (Ithaca, NY: Cornell University Press, 1989); Edith Wyschogrod, *Spirit in Ashes: Hegel, Heidegger, and Man-Made Mass Death* (New Haven, CT: Yale University Press, 1985).

8 Hans-Georg Gadamer, *Wahrheit und Methode* (Tübingen: J. C. B. Mohr, 1986), 5th rev. ed., 276ff.; Wayne Booth, *Modern Dogma and the Rhetoric of Assent* (Chicago: University of Chicago Press, 1974); Alasdair MacIntyre, *Whose Justice? Which Rationality?* (Notre Dame, IN: University of Notre Dame Press, 1988).

9 For example, see *Indigenous Peoples: A Global Quest for Justice* (London: Zed Books, 1987); L. S. Stavrianos, *Global Rift: The Third World Comes of Age* (New York: William Morrow, 1981); Ali Shari'ati, *Marxism and Other Western Fallacies: An Islamic Critique* (Berkeley: Mizan Press, 1980); and Gustavo Gutierrez, *The Power of the Poor in History* (Maryknoll, NY: Orbis Books, 1983), 169–233.

either the optimists who envisage progress as a myth with a moral, or nihilists for whom it is a myth without a moral?[10]

This is not a purely academic question. The destructive powers that science and technology provide to the military systems could decide it by annihilating the questioners. What is done to the poor, to native peoples, and to endangered species throughout the world could be done to all humankind. Modern dogmatic self-assertion is profoundly nihilistic, just as modern nihilism is irresponsibly dogmatic. Apocalypse has been instrumentally rationalized. If you think I exaggerate, recall the Holocaust, and visit Iron Mountain, your nearest Strategic Air Command, or Trident Submarine Base. Modern dogmatism is nihilistic.

Max Weber and Democratic Dogmatism

For Weber the distinction between value and fact is very much in line with a neo-Kantian separation by which counterfactual values are robbed of cognitive validity. Weber did this by first setting up instrumental rationality as normative for the rationalization process of modernity. He then stated how from the viewpoint of instrumental reason "the greater the value the greater its irrationality."[11] Weber is much closer to a Nietzschean void than the North American students of his sociology (especially in Talcott Parsons) have admitted.[12]

Weber explicitly distinguished the empirical sciences of action, such as sociology and history, from what he terms the "dogmatic disciplines . . . such as jurisprudence, logic, ethics, and esthetics, which seek to ascertain the 'true' and 'valid' meanings associated with the objects of their investigations."[13] Sociology and history are empirical and factual. Jurisprudence, ethics, aesthetics, and even logic are dogmatic. Within such a context, counterfactual moral values (that is, moral values that are grounded in the capacities of humans to transcend all factual injustices and immoralities), along with claims to truth and validity, are treated in dogmatic disciplines

---

[10] Franco Ferrarotti, *The Myth of Inevitable Progress* (Westport, CT: Greenwood Press, 1985).

[11] Max Weber, *Economy and Society,* trans. Guenther Roth and Claus Wittich (Berkeley: University of California Press, 1978), vol. I, 4–26, 85–86; vol II, 1116–17; on the rationalization process, cf. Weber's *Gesammelte Aufsätze zur Wissenschaftslehre* (Tübingen: J. C. B. Mohr, 1951), 2nd rev. ed., 471ff.

[12] Cf. Leo Strauss, *Natural Right and History* (Chicago: University of Chicago Press, 1953), 35–80, especially 65ff.; also Allan Bloom, *The Closing of the American Mind* (New York: Simon & Schuster, 1987), 151, 194ff.

[13] Weber, *Economy and Society,* vol. I, 4.

since they are dogmatic assertions. The methodological foundations of his social theory led Weber to an extrinsicist instrumentalism in social analysis. Social relations and institutions are primarily understood as structures of command and obedience, what Weber terms *Herrschaft* or domination. For Weber domination is intrinsic to social organization, the only relevant question is whether the domination is legitimate.

Modernity is constituted by the shift from traditional to rational forms of domination, from the established beliefs of ancient traditions to a "*belief* in the legality of enacted rules and the right of those elevated to authority under such rules to issue commands."[14] Weber believed we moderns have moved from a dogmatism of traditions to a dogmatism of conventionally established rules. Like traditional dogmatism, the dogmatism of conventionally established rules may be established by "consensus."[15]

The difference is that now the "consensus" is not mediated through hereditary or hierophanic agents, but by elected agents. We get to elect our *Herrschaften*, our controllers and commanders, and we call that freedom. The democratic character of the mediation, however, does not make the rules any less dogmatic. Their validity or truth are empirical only through the decisions establishing or grounding them. Truth or validity *(Geltung)* become decisionistic. Freedom in this context means either negating natural determinism in favor of conventional rules or moving from one type of consensus to another, from one conventional set of rules to another, from one dogmatism to another. If such is the case, it is difficult to avoid Nietzsche's farewell to the dialectic of Enlightenment and his move to a radically nihilistic self-assertion of the will to power.

> Ebensowenig wie diese Fragen der Religiösen gehen uns die Fragen der philosophischen Dogmatiker an, mögen sie nun Idealisten oder Materialisten oder Realisten sein. Sie allesamt sind darauf aus, uns zu einer Entscheidung auf Gebieten zu drängen, wo weder Glauben noch Wissen not tut. . . .[16]

Were the classic members of the Frankfurt School, with their Jewish memories, troubled by terrible insights into the concrete nihilism of modern

---

14 Ibid., vol. I, 212 ff.
15 Ibid., 457–63.
16 Nietzsche, *Menschliches, Allzumenschliches* (Stuttgart: Alfred Kröner, 1978), vol. 2, par. 16.

dogmatism? Granted, as Habermas remarks, the "dark" writers of the bourgeoisie appealed to Max Horkheimer. Granted, Horkheimer and Adorno's *Dialectic of Enlightenment* is an "odd book."[17] But in the name of reason and enlightenment, how were two German Jewish intellectuals to "make sense" of the terror of Holocaust that cast very deep dark shadows over Europe? Do the abstractions and formalism of communicative logic—as Fred Dallmayr claims—conjure up "a specter of solipsism"?[18] Does this specter block a rather fateful insight of Horkheimer and Adorno, that the horrors of Nazi Germany were not aberrations outside the pale of an enlightened modernity, but an apocalyptic fulfillment of its latent tendencies?

Only a thoroughly modern industrialized bureaucracy could have killed so many millions with such sterile efficiency. How are contemporary critics of modernity to make sense of the terrors so scientifically stored in nuclear weapons? How are they to deal with those modern deadly abuses of the medical arts not to heal human beings but to sterilize, to abort, and to euthanise them?

Could it be that "the palpable distortions" in modernity are not irrational deviations from its Enlightenment project? Could the "palpable distortions" be intrinsic to its "undeniable achievements"? These questions are implicit in Walter Benjamin's thesis that there is no document of civilization that is not also a document of barbarism, as well as his image of the angel of history with the terrible wreckage created by the storm we moderns call progress.[19]

Communicative Praxis as Normative

If we are troubled by these insights and questions we shall not misread Jürgen Habermas's reconstructions of critical theory as communicative action as sophisticated variations of solipsism or whistling in the dark. In my judgment

---

[17] Habermas, *The Philosophical Discourse of Modernity,* 106.

[18] Fred Dallmayr, *Polis and Praxis* (Cambridge: MIT Press, 1984), 250–53.

[19] Walter Benjamin, *Illuminations,* trans. Harry Zohn (New York: Schocken Books, 1978), 257–58: "This is how one pictures the angel of history. His face is turned toward the past. Where we perceive a chain of events [extrinsicism], he sees one single catastrophe which keeps piling wreckage upon wreckage and hurls it in front of his feet. The angel would like to stay, awaken the dead, and make whole what has been smashed. But a storm is blowing from Paradise; it has got caught in his wings with such violence that the angel can no longer close them. This storm irresistibly propels him into the future to which his back is turned, while the pole of debris before him grows skyward. This storm is what we call progress."

Habermas seeks to shift away from modern dogmatism while also avoiding its nihilism. I will first sketch just how he does this by showing how human questioning grounds his communicative action. Then I will indicate how a philosopher and theologian, Bernard Lonergan, developed a normative notion of human questioning as basic to all communicative praxis.

Jürgen Habermas's Performative Dialectics

How is reason practiced in such a way that reasonable judgments are not dogmatic in Weber's sense? I refer to communicative praxis rather than communicative action in order to indicate that the normative "action" is never totally objectified or expressed. Indeed, what is normative for human intelligence and reason is the praxis of raising ever further relevant questions. The root of dogmatism and nihilism in modernity, as in other epochs, is the fallacy of misplaced normativeness. It is the process of making the products of intelligence and reason as normative rather than the questioning praxis of intelligence and reason. We create something that is intelligent and marvelously rational, then we project onto it the powers of our own creative intelligence and reason. Religious, who recognize intelligence and reason as divine in origin, call this idolatry; secularists term it reification.

Communicative praxis within modernity must admit that praxis or performance can never be totally identified with its expressions in theory or narrative, and that institutionalizing enlightenment is always a communicative praxis in which reason is defined by the praxis of raising ever further relevant questions. Jürgen Habermas illustrates this in criticizing postmodern, totalizing critiques of modernity. Thomas McCarthy argues in his book, *The Philosophical Discourse of Modernity*, that "the defects of the Enlightenment can only be made good by further enlightenment." There are "performative contradictions" involved in using reason to negate reason:

> It is precisely the ambiguity of rationalization processes that has to be captured, the undeniable achievements as well as the palpable distortions; and this calls for a reconstructed dialectic of enlightenment rather than a totalized critique of it.[20]

How does Habermas "capture" the ambiguity of rationalization processes? He makes at least two major moves. First, he deconstructs the notion of totality realizing itself in the modern age, then he develops a dialectical

---

20 Habermas, *The Philosophical Discourse of Modernity*, xiv–xvii.

notion of communicative reason that can concretely and empirically transcend efforts to stifle or negate it.

History Is Human, Not Automatic

Habermas, as Martin Jay and others have indicated, has broken with his own earlier commitment, and with those of others in the Frankfurt School, to the concept of totality in Hegelian Marxism.[21] There is a "dogmatic version of the concept of a history of the human species" that presumes a *"unilinear, necessary, uninterrupted, and progressive development of a macrosubject."*[22] Habermas wants to develop "a weaker version" of the unity of history and the human species. In general he sees "society" as "a species undergoing social evolution." This is empirically accessible and can be developed without the intuitive or conceptual totality of rigid idealism and mechanical materialism.[23]

There are two significant features of this weaker version. First, adapting notions from Durkheim and Mead, Habermas holds for a growing "linguistification of the sacred" by which the "authoritarian and enforced" consensus of archaic norms dissolves, giving way to "the rationalization of worldviews, the universalization of law and morality, and accelerated processes of individuation."[24] The questions and concerns expressed in world religious traditions must be socially mediated and philosophically transformed in each generation, if the "semantic potential" of many values is not to be lost.[25] The "linguistification of the sacred," as Thomas McCarthy indicates, is reconstructed "as a learning process" in which communicative interaction leads to ever more active appropriations by the participants in mutual understandings, judgments, values.[26]

---

[21] Martin Jay, *Marxism and Totality: The Adventures of a Concept from Lákacs to Habermas* (Berkeley: University of California Press, 1984), 462–509.

[22] Jürgen Habermas, *Communication and the Evolution of Society,* trans. Thomas McCarthy (Boston: Beacon Press, 1979), 139.

[23] Jürgen Habermas, "Dogmatismus, Vernunft und Entscheidung—Zu Theorie und Praxis in der verwissenschaftlichen Zivilisation," in Jürgen Habermas, *Theorie und Praxis* (Frankfurt: Suhrkamp, 1971), 307–35; also his "Über das Subjekt der Geschichte: Diskussionsbemerkung zu falsch gestellten Alternativen," in his *Kultur und Kritik* (Frankfurt: Suhrkamp, 1973), 389–98.

[24] Habermas, *Theorie des kommunikativen Handelns* (Frankfurt: Suhrkamp, 1988), vol. II, 74ff.

[25] Habermas, "Metaphysik nach Kant," in K. Cramer et al., eds., *Theorie der Subjektivität* (Frankfurt: Suhrkamp, 1987), 431.

[26] Thomas McCarthy, introduction to his translation of vol. I of Jürgen Habermas, *The Theory of Communicative Action* (Boston: Beacon Press, 1984), xxv.

Second, Habermas does not leave the learning process in vague gener-
alities but shows how it has been socially and culturally differentiated in
the modern age. Modifying some categories from Weber, Habermas
claims that the specific contribution of modern cultures to the human
learning process can be seen in the "decentration" of worldviews, that is, in
the shift to a recognized pluralism of worldviews. Such decentration, however, does not lead to social or cultural anarchy or nihilism. For it is
accompanied by a decentering of consciousness that enables persons to
adopt different basic attitudes or orientations: (1) cognitive scientific-
instrumental, (2) the moral-practical, and (3) the aesthetic-practical
expressive. These basic attitudes are isomorphic (or heuristically relate) to
different domains of reality: (1) the objective domain of facts, (2) a nor-
matively regulated intersubjective realm, and (3) a subjective domain of
the self's inner experiences.[27]

But what happens when "rationalization of worldviews" becomes a
functionalist ideology? When "universalization of law and morality"
enforces particular laws or customs on others? When "individualization"
ends, not in an empowered inter-subjectivity but in monadic competition?

Communicative Reason Goes Beyond
Failures and Achievements

What enables Habermas to recover orientations, including self-critical orientations, that have not been realized? His interest in the modern classics in
philosophy and social theory is not primarily hermeneutical or historical
but dialectical. He has an acute sense of the further relevant question capable of exposing performative contradictions between an author's positions
and the concerns informing the communication. Reason and rationality are
not only tools of domination, of more or less violent struggle, of forced
control. Within rationalization processes are *non-coercive communicative*

---

27 Habermas, *The Philosophical Discourse of Modernity*, 110–13, 339–41; also his *The
Theory of Communicative Action*, vol. I, 234 ff. It would take us too far afield to
discuss how these differ from Habermas's earlier three quasi-transcendental interests in *Knowledge and Human Interests*. Have the psychoanalytic disciplines and
emancipatory interests now been displaced by the aesthetic? How do they transform Karl Popper's three worlds? They do have general institutional correlatives in
terms of (1) universities and scientific research institutes, (2) juridical and legal
professions, and (3) autonomous centers of art production and criticism. The significance of Bernard Lonergan's work is that he shows how the related and recurrent operations of human interiority (the third domain in Habermas) relates to the
first and second domains.

orientations that call into question whatever jeopardizes the learning processes constituted by persons raising further relevant questions.

In the pluralistic, decentered worldviews of modernity there is a center within humankind open to transcending or going beyond past and present failures and achievements. Habermas once stated this transcending empowerment in a reply to his critics:

> Marx wanted to capture the embodiments of unreason. In the same sense, we are also concerned today with the analysis of power constellations that suppress an *intention intrinsic to the rationality* of purposive action and linguistic understanding—the claim to reason announced in the teleological and intersubjective structures of social reproduction themselves—and that allow it to take effect only in a distorted manner. Again and again this claim [to communicative reason] is silenced; and yet in fantasies and deeds it develops a *stubbornly transcending* power, because it is renewed with each act of unconstrained understanding, with each moment of living together in solidarity, of successful individuation, of saving emancipation.[28]

The desire for intelligence and reason, the troubled and struggling intention toward uncoerced and genuine communication is as close to the center of Habermas's dialectics as anything he has yet, to my knowledge, articulated.

The emancipatory interest in communicative praxis is anything but dogmatic self-assertion. It is one with "the stubbornly transcending power" of communicative reason. It can be traced in intersubjective self-correcting processes of learning, and some of these traces are institutionalized within modernity, and so can subvert the totalizing identification of power and reason. Dogmatism and nihilism confuse the normativeness of *universalistischen Fragestellungen* with the long since abandoned validity ascribed to particular answers, theories, and systems.[29]

The totalizing critiques of modernity depend upon fictitious "normative intuitions" *(normativen Intuitionen)* that become trapped, if I understand Habermas's argument correctly, in "performative contradictions" of (1) by projecting pictures or figures of undamaged intersubjectivity or necessary macrosubjects, or progressive competitive system expansions, and yet (2) are

---

[28] In John Thompson and David Held, eds., *Habermas: Critical Debates* (Cambridge: MIT Press, 1982), 221 [emphasis mine].

[29] Habermas, *The Philosophical Discourse of Modernity*, 408, n. 28. Regarding the claims of classical metaphysics, see below.

unable to recognize the stubbornly transcending power of communicative reason to emancipate us from instrumental totalitarian objectifications and totalizing, inclusive ideologies by means of uncoerced insights, judgments, and communicative actions.[30]

Fred Dallmayr, among others, thinks Habermas passes too quickly over the philosophy of the subject into communicative action theory. Had Habermas deconstructed the Cartesian subject, with its self-asserting replacement of both the conscious immediacy of questioning and discursive knowing with *thinking*, he may have been able to pursue more thoroughly his criticisms of the dogmatism in Kant, Hegel, and Marx. Communicative reason, raising ever further relevant questions, articulates the heuristic dynamics of Habermas's formal-pragmatic relations with their basic attitudes and objective, social, and subjective worlds in a way that avoids the pitfalls of reifying language, thereby emphasizing Habermas's own concrete references to speech acts and intentions.[31]

Working out the dialectical transitions from the philosophy of the subject to communicative action would also exploit the heuristic praxis orientations in such sources as Piaget and Kohlberg. As Piaget analyzes the growth process in a series of adaptations and mediations, so the social intersubjective sets of self-correcting processes of learning (cognitive, moral, aesthetic, religious) continually differentiate into sets of adaptations and mediations that are world-disclosive and world-transformative. Working through the dialectical transitions from modern philosophies of the subject to communicative praxis would also indicate more adequately how individual freedom and universal solidarity are not contradictory (as they tend to be cast in liberal capitalism and socialist collectivism) but profoundly harmonious.[32]

---

30 Ibid., 336ff. This argument expresses insights analogous to those of Anthony Giddens on the duality of structure, and distanciation from bureaucratic control, in his *The Constitution of Society* (Berkeley: University of California Press, 1984), 5–40, 281–354.

31 Habermas, *The Theory of Communicative Action,* vol. 1, 279–337; on the questions raised, see Fred Dallmayr, *Polis and Praxis,* 224–53; also Dallmayr's "Critical Epistemology Criticized," in his *Beyond Dogma and Despair: Toward a Critical Phenomenology of Politics* (Notre Dame, IN: University of Notre Dame Press, 1981), 246–93; also the criticisms raised by Thomas McCarthy, Henning Ottmann, and John Thompson, along with Habermas's responses, in *Habermas: Critical Debates,* 57–161, 219–83.

32 It seems to me in reading Habermas in terms of his *performative questioning,* it is toward such an articulation of rational praxis that he is heading. Making this more explicit would, for example, answer some of the questions posed by Anthony Giddens in his "Reason without Revolution?" in Richard J. Bernstein, ed., *Habermas*

Moreover, this would also highlight a central concern of Habermas. He clearly affirms that there is no normative *content* to modernity, whether it be intuitions, concepts, systems, rules, axioms, or institutions, but rather that the effectively free exercise of intelligence and reason is normative in social and cultural interaction. Precisely this concern could be missed in his formulation of the formal pragmatic relations. He both corrects idealist tendencies to separate the expressive and imaginal from the rational and conceptual and the naturalist tendencies to collapse them. However, to date he only seems to recognize the non-objectivated *environment* or *Umwelt* in terms of human moral-practical spontaneity (*Moral* as differentiated from *Recht*) and sensual spontaneity.[33]

As Thomas McCarthy and others indicate, this concedes too much to Weber's *Zweckrationalität*, and tends to hand over the natural sciences to empiricist and instrumentalist philosophies. How does that differ from the "strategic retreats" that the human sciences have been making vis-à-vis empiricism? Are not the instances now multiplying where "the stubbornly transcending power" of communicative reason subverts the empiricist and instrumentalist misreadings of empirical science? Moreover, if cognitive spontaneity does not operate in all three spheres of human activity, what besides force can settle disputes in the cognitive-empirical sphere?[34]

What Habermas, in speaking of Benjamin and Peukert, calls "the communicative context of a universal historical solidarity" undercuts the facile misunderstanding of communicative praxis as a new and improved "paradigm" or "model," replacing older ones the way we replace television sets: The knowing subject (with theories of consciousness and presence) was replaced by the producing subject (with forces and relations of production), which is now replaced by a "new and improved" communicative action (with uncoercive consensus and universal pragmatics). Communicative praxis is not new. Like human subjecthood or agency, it is a set of human actions and relations that is not identified with the "theories" or

---

and Modernity (Cambridge, MA: MIT Press, 1985), 111ff. Working through the dialectical transitions from the modern philosophies of the subject to communicative reason would also strengthen Habermas's corrections to Kohlberg's stages. For relations between Lonergan's work and both Piaget and Kohlberg, cf. Walter Conn, *Conscience: Development and Self-Transcendence* (Birmingham: Religious Education Press, 1981).

[33] Habermas, *The Theory of Communicative Action*, vol. 1, 236ff.

[34] *Habermas: Critical Debates*, 57–115; *Habermas and Modernity*, 177–91.

"concepts" that we form about them. It is a praxis that occurs before we know about it, indeed it is a praxis through which we come to know it.[35]

Bernard Lonergan's Dialectics of Reason

The philosopher of science Patrick Heelan shows how Bernard Lonergan's work in cognitional theory provides terms and relations needed for an understanding of quantum mechanics, and the structure of physical science generally, as communicative languages.[36] The interest in empirical science is not primarily control or instrumental domination, but rather questioning natural events, no longer as those events are mediated by unaided sense data, but through complex explanatory languages of instrumental measurement. While this certainly differentiates the learning process enormously, empirical sciences in the modern age are examples *par excellence* of research communities engaged in raising ever further relevant questions and correcting previous errors. Indeed, it is precisely the empiricist and positivist misunderstandings of the empirical sciences that alienate economic and political policies relative to scientific and technological projects.[37]

Bernard Lonergan's *Insight: A Study of Human Understanding* is unequaled in its articulation of the questioning dynamism of human intelligence.[38] He relates intelligent spontaneity to the spontaneity of affective and moral desires. Ethics is related to intelligence. No one has to attend school to acquire questions, to experience the questioning that spontaneously desires to understand what one is sensing, perceiving, or imagining. There is a spontaneous intersubjectivity to illocutionary acts. Humans spontaneously question one another's, or their own, understandings of experience. We want not only to understand but to understand correctly. We are not satis-

---

35 Habermas, *The Philosophical Discourse of Modernity,* 14ff.

36 Patrick Heelan, *Quantum Mechanics and Objectivity: A Study of the Physical Philosophy of Werner Heisenberg* (The Hague: Martinus Nijhoff, 1965). This has been further elaborated by a student of Heelan, Patrick Byrne, in "Lonergan on the Foundations of the Theories of Relativity," in Matthew Lamb, ed., *Creativity and Method: Essays in Honor of Bernard Lonergan* (Milwaukee, WI: Marquette University Press, 1982), 477–94.

37 David F. Noble, *Forces of Production: A Social History of Industrial Automation* (New York: Alfred Knopf, 1984); Seymour Melman, *Profits without Production* (New York: Alfred Knopf, 1983); Joshua S. Goldstein, *Long Cycles: Prosperity and War in the Modern Age* (New Haven, CT: Yale University Press, 1988).

38 Bernard Lonergan, *Insight: A Study of Human Understanding* (New York, Philosophical Library, 1957).

fied with thinking—we want to know, to give reasons why our understanding is correct. Habermas expresses this desire for correct understanding:

> Thus an interpreter cannot become clear about the semantic content of an expression independently of the action contexts in which participants react to the expression with a "yes" or a "no" or an abstention. And he does not understand this yes/no position if he cannot make clear to himself the implicit reasons that move the participants to take the positions they do . . . reasons of such a nature that they cannot be described in the attitude of a third person. . . . One can understand reasons only to the extent that one understands why they are or they are not sound.[39]

Unlike Lonergan, Habermas does not explore the spontaneously operative praxis of questions for understanding and questions for judgment.[40]

Judgment leads to the moral-practical spontaneity that questions whether something is worth doing, with the personal and interpersonal deliberations and evaluations that can give reasons for this or that course of action. No one needs a degree to wonder and to raise questions from experience for understanding, from understanding for validity and truth, from validity and truth for genuine values and goods. The communicative praxis of intelligence, reason, and responsibility is the performance of raising ever further relevant questions.[41]

The spontaneity of intelligence and reason precedes any distinction between one's self and others. That to which Lonergan calls our attention is anything but the objectified "subject" or "consciousness" or "presence" described in the modern theories of the same. Habermas perceives the shortcomings of all such theories, whether they be totalitarian objectifications or all-inclusive totalizing critiques. His concern for "performative contradiction" is articulated in Lonergan's analysis of how our spontaneous sensitivity,

---

[39] Habermas, *The Theory of Communicative Action*, vol. I, 115–16.

[40] If Habermas were to explore the implications of judgment, as Lonergan has, he would be able to break more decisively with his Kantian presuppositions, see Giovanni Sala, SJ, "The A Priori in Human Knowledge: Kant's Critique of Pure Reason and Lonergan's Insight," *The Thomist* 40 (1976): 179–221. The exploration of judgment is also central in understanding the question of God, see Sala, *Kant und die Frage nach Gott* (Berlin: Walter de Gruyter, 1990).

[41] Bernard Lonergan, *Insight: A Study of Human Understanding* (New York: Philosophical Library, 1957), 207–17, 289–98, 607ff. Also his "Cognitional Structure," in the *Collected Works of Bernard Lonergan*, vol. 4 (Toronto: University of Toronto Press, 1988), 205–22.

intelligence, reason, and evaluative activities are normed, not by extrinsic rules or axioms or principles, but by our spontaneous questioning that seeks to be attentive (sensitivity), intelligent (understanding), reasonable (truth), and responsible (value). In their disagreements, humans call attention to data overlooked, to alternate ways of understanding, to evidence or warrants not given, to values or goods not chosen. This self-correcting process of learning, as Lonergan indicates, is neither dominative nor dogmatically self-assertive.

Such intelligence and reason as questioning is anything but an absolute Geist intuiting absolute concepts. The related and recurrent operations of communicative praxis are the open and normative patterns of human freedom. While we all are inattentive, stupid, unreasonable, and irresponsible at times, we effectively expand our freedom when we attend to the questioning desires for attentiveness, intelligence, reasonableness, and responsibility.

Not only does this communicative praxis constitute life worlds, it also constitutes, in ever more differentiated manners, the sciences. Michael H. McCarthy has demonstrated that the totalizing orientations within modernity can be traced to a failure of philosophical reflection to understand how the emerging empirical sciences performatively broke with the Aristotelian ideal of certain knowledge of necessary causes. Descartes attributed necessity and certainty to thinking subjectivity. The positivistic misunderstanding of the empirical sciences is, as Habermas has remarked, related to traditional, classicist ontology.[42] The pivotal role of judgment was collapsed into a curious type of Platonic dualism, now recast in terms of body versus mind, sensations versus ideas. Since no human ideas (even the *ego cogito*) could survive Descartes's universal doubt, the empiricists simply transferred *necessity* and *certainty* to sensations or perceptions. This set the stage for the interminable modern debates between empiricists and idealists.[43]

The turn to communicative praxis is part of postempiricist philosophies of science, which, in tune with critical theory, break with the absolutizing concentration on necessity and certainty. Unfortunately, modern philosophies of science, while fixated on a basically classicist ideal of certain knowledge of necessary causes, tended to concur with the modern moral philosophies that rejected the Aristotelian theory of the virtues,

42 Habermas, *Knowledge and Human Interest*, 302–3.]
43 Michael H. McCarthy, *The Crisis of Philosophy* (Albany: State University of New York Press, 1990).

with its development of practical judgments in contingently historical ways. The judgments of science, as postempiricist philosophies of science indicate, are more like the conditioned universality of moral judgments *(phronesis)* than the deductivist universality of necessary and unconditioned axioms or principles.[44]

The postempiricist philosophies of science clearly reject the ideals of necessity and certainty informing the quest for a complete and coherent theoretical articulation of reason. This would make reason into a monistic absolute, as if reason could be completely expressed, as if all questions would be fully answered. These philosophies also reject the inference from the radical incompleteness of human rationality that reason must be totally criticized. Arational relativism or irrational anarchism, proposed by many postmoderns, is an inference premised on the mistaken assumption that if rationality exists, it must be capable of complete and coherent theoretic purity. Instead, postempiricist philosophies affirm the praxis of reason as the performance of raising ever further relevant questions within communities engaged in empirical, hermeneutical, and/or dialectical inquiry in order to articulate coherently—yet always incompletely—both the answers discovered by their questioning praxis, as well as the heuristic relations within these communities of inquiry and other forms of the questioning praxis of reason (e.g., the life-world of everyday common sense living, aesthetic spheres, moral, religious).[45]

The universality of communicative praxis is not constituted by intuitions, concepts, theories, axioms, or principles. Nor is it mediated from "the top down." No theory or system can coherently *and* completely express rational praxis. It is a universality constituted by attentive, intelligent, rational, and responsible communicative praxis, and is mediated through the plurality of persons and communities communicating and questioning. Moreover, this universality is coherent but always incomplete, requiring openness to further relevant questions. Such openness is

---

[44] See among others Richard Bernstein, *Beyond Objectivism and Relativism: Science, Hermeneutics, and Praxis* (Philadelphia: University of Pennsylvania Press, 1983); Alasdair MacIntyre, *After Virtue: A Study in Moral Theory* (Notre Dame, IN: University of Notre Dame Press, 1981); idem, *Whose Justice? Which Rationality?* (Notre Dame, IN: University of Notre Dame Press, 1988); David Tracy, *Plurality and Ambiguity* (San Francisco: Harper & Row, 1987).

[45] See Matthew Lamb, "The Dialectic of Theory and Praxis within Paradigm Analysis" in Hans Küng and David Tracy, eds., *Paradigm Change in Theology* (New York: Crossroad, 1989), 63–109.

not the fiction of a Cartesian universal doubt, for questions are relevant to data, and occur within multiple contexts of communication and belief.[46]

One need not read Descartes to experience one's own consciousness, Dilthey or Gadamer to experience one's desire to understand, Lonergan to desire to understand correctly, or Habermas to desire genuine communication. Communicative praxis is grounded in what Habermas terms "the stubbornly transcending power," and Lonergan the desire raising ever further relevant questions in ongoing self-correcting processes of learning. This is what is normative. It is not dogmatically asserted. Lonergan explicitly invites his readers to verify in their own performance the activities and operations he derives from human questioning spontaneity. We read these philosophers to understand the *performative contradictions* between human intersubjective spontaneity and its distortions and derailments.

Like Habermas, Lonergan called for a second enlightenment to carry forward the advances of the first:

> The Enlightenment—it becomes just the first Enlightenment if a second is recognized—was carried socially and culturally. Socially by the movement that would sweep away the remnants of feudalism and a lingering absolutism by proclaiming liberty, fraternity, equality. Culturally by the triumph of Newton, who did for mechanics what Euclid had done for geometry and who led philosophers to desert rationalism and swell the ranks of empiricists.[47]

While the empiricism and positivism of the first Enlightenment may still dominate, Lonergan traces the emergence of what he terms the second enlightenment, which, from its cultural origin in the relativizing of Euclidean geometry, relativity theories, and quantum mechanics, has moved on to challenge empiricism and positivism in economics, politics, and the deductivist pretensions of both empiricism and idealism in philosophy.

> Of itself this second enlightenment is culturally significant. But it may have as well a social mission. Just as the first enlightenment had

---

46 Lonergan, *Insight,* 703–18.

47 Bernard Lonergan, "The Second Enlightenment," in his *A Third Collection* (New York: Paulist Press, 1985), 63–65. The non-Euclidean geometries indicate how the quest for necessary and deductively certain principles was mistaken: "from being regarded as the unique deduction of necessary truth from self-evident principles (e.g., in Kant) it became just one of many possible geometric systems deduced from freely chosen postulates."

its carrier in the transition from feudal to bourgeois society, so the second may find a role and task in offering hope and providing leadership to the masses alienated by large establishments under bureaucratic management.[48]

Theology and Public Realms

There are many implications in any dialogue between critical theory and theology for a theology of the public realm. I shall sketch three.

Communicative Praxis is Never Dominative

Helmut Peukert has shown that what is new in the twentieth century is not the use of reason to critique reason, which belongs to the tradition of enlightenment. What is new, and what Benjamin and other early critical theorists wrestled with, was an inverse insight: Enlightened reason cannot measure up to the consequences of its actions.[49]

For very understandable reasons deriving from the European wars of religion, there are two fundamental presuppositions on which most Western modern philosophers agree, whether they are conservative, liberal, or radical. The first presupposition is that natural and historical realities are ultimately conflictive, as though reality is made up of contradictory forces contending for dominance. The second is that knowledge is the power to control, a learning of secrets in order to enforce order and secure dominance. Little wonder, then, that Max Weber thought social organization always involved domination *(Herrschaft)*. Habermas also espouses this, at least in regard to the empirical-analytic sciences. They are supposedly informed by instrumentalist interests in technically dominating nature since "the human species secures its existence in systems of social labor and self-assertion through violence," while he differentiates communication and individuation from such dominative interest.[50]

It seems to me that neither Judaism nor Christianity can accept these two fundamental presuppositions. God's creative act is not an act of violence and domination—indeed, the Hebrew creation narratives repudiated the

---

[48] Ibid.

[49] Helmut Peukert, "Praxis Universaler Solidarität," in Edward Schillebeeckx, OP, ed., *Mystik und Politik: Theologie im Ringen um Geschichte und Gesellschaft* (Mainz: Matthias Grünewald, 1988), 172–85. On inverse insights, see Lonergan, *Insight*, 19–26, 387, 687–89.

[50] Habermas, *Knowledge and Human Interests*, 313; also Thomas McCarthy, *The Critical Theory of Jürgen Habermas* (Cambridge: MIT Press, 1979), 53ff.

violent cosmogonies of the surrounding empires. The empires and superpowers of history have become what they are through force and violence so it is hardly surprising that their visions of world birth would be violent. Quite different are the narratives of the victims of empires and superpowers. Creation is good, creation nourishes us, and metaphors of gardening, not killing, are central. Indeed, Jewish and Christian revelations intensify intersubjective communication infinitely. God speaks and the universe comes into being. Humans emerge and are called to respond in faith and love, not in violence and force, which latter are the results of sin.

Insofar as religious faith is a knowledge born of love, it is important that the wisdom of such faith engage in communicative praxis with the sciences and technologies that, unfortunately, seem urgently in need of a healing transformation away from the fears and aggressions engendering them.[51] But this "insofar as" has to be stressed. For just as there is needed a dialectic of enlightenment that differentiates the genuine exercise of reason from the abuse of reason to subject nature and persons as instruments to another, so there is needed a dialectic of religious experience that differentiates genuine religious praxis from the abuse of religion to dominate and control. As Helmut Peukert indicates, only such a mutually critical exercise of reason and religion can foster the collaboration between the sciences and religious or theological scholarship adequate to contemporary challenges.[52]

Christian Doctrine

Theology will not be able to aid a genuine dialectic of enlightenment if it continues to internalize the caricatures of itself that the Enlightenment first portrayed. How often we hear, for example, a dominative and "dogmatic" reconstruction of Christianity's own dogmas. Is it not curious that whenever theologians uncritically assimilate an imperial culture around them, they marvelously discover how the origins of Christian doctrine in the Great Councils were equally if not more imperial. Theologians still

---

51 Matthew Lamb, "Christianity with the Political Dialectics of Community and Empire," in N. Biggar, J. Scott, and W. Schweiker, eds., *Cities of Gods: Faith, Politics and Pluralism in Judaism, Christianity and Islam* (New York: Greenwood, 1986), 73–100. On the relevance of this to Habermas's work, see Steven Lukes, "Of Gods and Demons: Habermas and Practical Reason," in J. Thompson and D. Held, eds., *Habermas: Critical Debates* (Cambridge, MA: MIT Press, 1982), 134–48, 254ff.

52 Helmut Peukert, "Über die Zukunft von Bildung," *Frankfurter Hefte* 6 (1984): 129–37. Also Lamb, "The Dialectic of Theory and Praxis within Paradigm Analysis," 86ff.

refer to the Imperial Church of the Constantinian epoch and completely identify the Nicean confession of faith with that Imperialism. Such theologians accept with minor reservations the picture of events provided by the first of all self-important Christian court theologians, Eusebius of Caesarea. Eusebius was more interested in power than in orthodoxy. In light of the first Enlightenment's prejudices, modern theologians, who accept Eusebius's distortions, negate orthodoxy as intrinsically "dogmatic" in the pejorative sense, that is, as a use of faith to control and dominate.[53]

Such reconstructions illustrate the distorted communication with the past, with the men and women who strove to live their faith in Christ Jesus as intelligently and responsibly as they could. It weakens those who strive to do so today, for they are not provided with the social power that comes from a realization of our solidarity in the Body of Christ. But, just as the distorted pictures of the Enlightenment can be overcome by the self-correcting learning processes of communicative reasoned praxis, so ongoing theological scholarship, attuned to the dialectics of enlightenment and of religion, can begin to indicate what a jejune and distorted reconstruction of orthodoxy that is.

Athanasius was hardly a court theologian. Ejected many times from his diocese and strong in his support for the thousands of devout Christian communities of study and prayer, he realized that the God revealed in the life, death, and resurrection of Jesus Christ is not the Imperial One, with Son and Spirit as imperial emanations subordinate to Father. No, orthodoxy confessed the God of Jesus Christ as a unity of Consubstantial Persons.[54] Indeed, it was within the orthopraxis of fervent local churches, out of which the monastic communities of women and men emerged, that Athanasius found the graced foundations of orthodoxy.[55] The work of Bernard Lonergan demonstrates

---

[53] Variations on this theme are widespread. For a recent version, see Elaine Pagels's *Adam, Eve, and the Serpent* (New York: Random House, 1988). Pagels turns Augustine into an "imperial church" theologian, a claim she can make only by ignoring the dialectics Augustine elaborated between empire and church in *The City of God.* Augustine, like Athanasius, realized that overcoming imperialism was the task of all humankind graced by God's Incarnation carried on in the communion of the church. Pelagius, like Eusebius, simply underestimated the power of imperialism. Pagels seems to do so as well.

[54] Aloys Grillmeier, *Christ in the Christian Tradition,* trans. John Bowden (Atlanta, GA: John Knox Press, 1975), 250–71, 308ff. for a differentiation of the imperial church from the Nicean faith.

[55] See Athanasius's *Life of Anthony,* which had a profound impact on both Orthodox and Catholic Christianity. Also Armand Veilleux, *The Pachomian Koinonia,* 3 vols.

the need to recover the intellectual, moral, and religious orthopraxis that has been the matrix out of which genuine orthodoxy lives through the ages.[56]

Secularism and Abuse of Reason?

Does Modern Secularism Project Onto Faith Its Abuse of Reason?

Among the many tasks of a dialectic of enlightenment, or a second enlightenment, is the recognition that religious faiths and practices do not by definition lack intelligence and reason. A theology for the public realm, especially here in the United States, will be effective only if it overcomes the deep cultural tendency to treat religion at best as utilitarian ("useful for the common weal") and at worst as a type of occult or public fanaticism. The sociology of religion is hardly helpful in this task, as long as it maintains the Weberian dichotomy between fact and value, between cognitive and ethical orientations. The charismatic and the apocalyptic are often used in ways that blunt, by being wrapped in fanatical connotations, the serious questions they pose to the culture. Like religion generally, charismatic is either benign and so useful, or malignant and so fanatical.

This distortion masks, however, a deeper problem within the Western Enlightenment. Confronted with the tragic wars of religion in Europe, Enlightenment intellectuals tended to criticize religion rather than war. Just as religious truth was equated with domination, so all truth remains linked with power and violence. A consequence remains the terribly violent orientation in all national public realms.[57] Indeed, modern industrial-

---

(Kalamazoo, MI: Cistercian Publications, 1980) for important writings from the Egyptian monasteries in which Athanasius sought refuge when he was persecuted by the imperial forces. Note that the communities of monks and nuns did not understand themselves as fleeing from a corrupt Church that had compromised with empire (pace von Harnack et al.), rather they understood themselves as in communion with the local churches genuinely following Christ. Cf. Armand Veilleux, "The Monastery as a School of Orthopraxis," not yet published. W. H. C. Frend, *The Rise of Christianity* (Philadelphia: Fortress Press, 1984), 423, 477–88, illustrates an uncritical assimilation of Eusebius of Caesarea, and a failure to understand the issues at stake both in monasticism and in the Trinitarian controversies.

56 Bernard Lonergan, *De Deo Trino* (Rome: Gregorian University Press, 1964) and *De Verbo Incarnato* (Rome: Gregorian University Press, 1965). These Latin works, along with English translations, will be included within the twenty-two volume edition of the *Collected Works of Bernard Lonergan*, which the University of Toronto Press has begun publishing.

57 Anthony Giddens's *The Nation State and Violence* (Berkeley: University of California Press, 1985); also his *The Consequences of Modernity* (Stanford: Stanford University

ized war-making far overshadows all previous forms of organized violence. This is the terribly apocalyptic significance of Holocaust, Hiroshima, and the World Wars. The Middle Ages and Renaissance had a successor, the Modern Age. Will modernity have a successor? For the first time in world history, humankind's biological survival is questionable. The intelligent and very reasonable insights into this shadow side of modernity, the instrumentalization of apocalyptic evil, are misunderstood as negations of reason because the normativeness of reason is wrongly identified with necessary, unilinear progress in a struggle for survival.

The modern age did not invent communicative praxis. No one culture has it copyrighted. There are achievements in wisdom, in moral goodness, and in common sense that any enlightenment would overlook at its own peril. The myth of necessary unilinear progress in the struggle for survival is not secularized Jewish and Christian salvation history. Rather it stems from Euclidean and Newtonian quantification of all reality in the empiricism of seventeenth-century Europe, linked with the Hobbesian instrumentalization of intelligence as a tool in the supposed war of all against all.[58]

It is still difficult for philosophers and theologians to understand the genial insights of an Augustine and Aquinas regarding eternity and time, especially given the tendency to regard the former as either a phenomenal or noumenal duration. Moderns wrongly stretch apocalyptic metaphors onto their own grids of duration and extension (as, for example, Newton's chronology of Daniel's apocalyptic prophecies). Indeed, there are many rather central theological doctrines in which contemporary theologians continue to misconstrue premodern classics.[59]

We are all moderns and, if we are to take the self-correcting processes of learning within scholarship seriously, we have much to learn from the men and women of past ages. Communicative praxis is not restricted to the present generation. Every age and culture has its mistakes, biases, and sins.

Press, 1990). There is also the extensive work of Michel Foucault on the modern equation of knowledge and dominative power.

[58] Amos Funkenstein, *Theology and the Scientific Imagination from the Middle Ages to the Seventeenth Century* (Princeton, NJ: Princeton University Press, 1986). The author's scholarship on Aquinas is inadequate. Cf. Michael Buckley, SJ, *At the Origins of Modern Atheism* (New Haven, CT: Yale University, 1987).

[59] Sir Isaac Newton, *Opera quae exstant Omnia* (Stuttgart-Bad Cannstatt: F. Frommann Verlag, 1964); also his *Theological Manuscripts*, selected and edited with introduction by H. McLachlan (Liverpool: University Press, 1950).

Communicative praxis recognizes how cooperative consensus has to be universal if it is not going to self-destruct. One of the errors of modernity has been to misconstrue traditions and the past as no more than dominative and benighted authoritarian repression out of which modernity emerges. As Lonergan remarked, "any present is powerful in the measure that past achievement lives on in it."[60]

Modernity fails to discern the normative achievements of the past and to differentiate them from the errors, biases, and sins. For example, Habermas reads Durkheim and develops a notion of "the linguistification of the sacred" as a process of learning. By a very different route Lonergan discovered that what Augustine meant by *desiderium animi*, the desire of mind, and Thomas Aquinas meant by *lumen intellectus agentis*, the light of intelligence in act, was the human capacity to raise ever further relevant questions. That capacity was healed and intensified, not dogmatically broken or distorted, by religious faith. Aquinas structures the whole of theology as ongoing questions. Theodor Adorno glimpsed this judging from the quotation at the beginning of this paper.

Why did an Augustine or Aquinas understand their faith in Jesus Christ as the incarnate Son of God as a healing intensification of their intelligence and reason? For Augustine, it was the only way hate and domination in the imperial cities of man, which so tragically used intelligence and reason to destroy, could avoid extinguishing the quest for wisdom and intelligence. For Aquinas, the barbarity of evil in human history is only adequately met by the light of faith and agapic love. Humankind can only excel in the intellectual and moral virtues if these were strengthened and intensified by the theological virtues. We are back at the consequences of the use of reason to destroy reason. What else is the Holocaust? What else is the nuclear arms race? What else accounts for the millions of abortions in modernity?

The Theodicy Question

Habermas seems to overlook in Benjamin just this struggle with the consequences of using reason to negate the reason of others. Is it not true that the theodicy problem *as it is posed in modernity* admits of no intelligent and rational answer?

---

60 Bernard Lonergan, "Dialectic of Authority," in his *Third Collection* (New York: Paulist Press, 1985), 5. Lonergan's way of posing the dialectic of authority is fundamental, in my judgment, for a proper understanding of communicative praxis.

There can be no intelligent and rational answer for several reasons. First, in modernity intelligence and rationality are distorted into conceptualistic instruments of all sorts. This distortion was then, as it was by Leibniz and others, projected into infinity as a divine intelligence and reason. The theodicy problematic put modern theologians in the dilemma of either denying the very real suffering of history or of claiming that the leap of faith is irrational. Only if they questioned the very presuppositions of the conception of intelligence and reason in modern theodicy are they able to avoid the dilemma.

Second, the truncation of modern reason (which has a prehistory— Lonergan on how Kant's critique is not of pure reason but of reason à la Scotus) led to a conflation of logic and conceptualist theories that led to the conceptualist philosophies of the subject, consciousness, and unilinear progress we have already discussed. The appeal was forevermore comprehensive logical concepts or all-embracing theories. With the collapse of these pretensions, the postmodernists, whom Habermas criticizes, collapse reason too quickly into Nietzschean nihilism.

Third, Jewish and Christian prophetic and mystical traditions reveal an answer to the massively concrete histories of human suffering. But it is not a human conceptual answer. Any human and historical theory that made such claims should be denounced as idolatrous blasphemy in the presence of the dead and suffering. *No mere theory can console the suffering, no concept can raise the dead.* Peukert indicates how this is implied in Benjamin's very Jewish demand for an openness of the past (as well as the present and future) to messianic interruption. Messianic expectation is also present in Johann B. Metz's insistence on the eschatological proviso and the apocalyptic interruption of all modern myths of time entombing humankind in a closed and endless duration. The answer to the massively concrete histories of evil, oppression, and suffering—the only adequate answer—far exceeds all human hearts and minds.[61]

The *theological* affirmation that God's infinite understanding and love alone is the answer breaks the epistemic cynicism of modernity, a cynicism that claims that intelligence and love are merely more cunning weapons or tools in some great universal struggle for existence. Moreover, the theological

---

[61] Johann B. Metz, "Productive Noncontemporaneity," in Jürgen Habermas, ed., *Observations on the Spiritual Situation of the Age* (Cambridge: M.I.T. Press, 1984), 169–77. For another perspective, see Terrence Tilley, *The Evils of Theodicy* (Washington, DC: Georgetown University Press, 1990).

affirmation that God alone is capable of transforming evil into good, death into life, sin into grace is not cheap consolation or opium, but a confession as well to the enormous evil and suffering from which we must be redeemed.

Political theology, as Metz understands it, unites the mystical and the prophetic. The mystical and mysterious assertion "God is the Answer to massive evil and suffering," does not induce apathy, but informs strong and clear prophetic denunciations of evil and calls to decisive action with and for the oppressed. The prophetic and mystical traditions of Judaism and Christianity, and the concrete practices of discipleship through the ages, keep alive the faith, hope, and agapic love that inform a non-instrumental compassion and solidarity. These few reflections might at least suggest how we humans are not alone in struggling with these terrible questions.

Theologies for Public Realms

The public realm in the United States is in danger of becoming an abstract, conceptualized universality. In such a public realm the participants are led to believe that the plurality of their traditions, races, genders, and religions requires that they intellectually bracket those particularities, with their truth claims, for the sake of "civil" public discourse. The public realm is constituted, then, in two moves. First there are the efforts to develop abstract symbols, axioms, principles, or whatever minimum on which all could agree. Differences are abstracted out of melting pot, for they are conflictual by definition. Second, there are ground rules for civil and legal negotiations of those differences that particular pressure groups are unwilling to bracket. Such an abstract universality, with its social, civil, and state formalism, is extrinsicist and dogmatic. The rules of the game, the procedures of the public realm, demand compromise and a relentless privatization of those cherished beliefs and values that disrupt a smooth functioning of the public realm.

It is misleading to imagine that there is only one public realm in the United States, and that we can develop "a" theology for it: That would be to approach the question with either deductive or inductive conceptualism. I find too much of that approach still operative, often without advertence, in works on world religions and in public discourse.[62] Communicative

---

62 For example, Paul Knitter, *No Other Name* (Maryknoll, NY: Orbis Books, 1985). Knitter seeks to find an orientation agreeable to all religions. This, it seems to me, is an inductively impoverishing abstraction. Ecclesiocentrism is immediately abandoned, yet it is only in and through religious institutions that the long-term dialogue of world religions occurs.

praxis would suggest that attention to all relevant questions within one's immediate contexts is a proper starting point. This means that the theologies of the public realms will indeed have a universal significance, but only as mediated in and through the many communities of religious discourse and ecclesial action operative in the many public realms constituting our society and culture. The universality of the many public realms is mediated in and through the particularities of the many communities. The discourse that would make this concretely possible has hardly begun, and must contend with the impoverishing abstractions fed by the communication media.

Religious truth claims cannot be bracketed, anymore than faith should be cut off from intelligence in theological discourse. This requires that truth questions be clearly and consistently differentiated from domination, violence, and force. If such concrete truth claims are ignored in theology, then theology becomes as privatized as religion is in our culture.

No wonder, then, that there is a very strong tendency, especially in the United States, towards an individualism that is excessively monadic, if not egophanic, with an accompanying failure to understand the vast differences between *intentional* communities within institutionalized traditions, on the one hand, and voluntary associations of like-minded monads on the other. The public realms in the United States are particularly vulnerable to the misunderstandings that cast synagogues, churches, or mosques in the same lot as clubs and other voluntarily associated pressure groups. This privatizes religion drastically, since it is taken for granted that, in areas where religious traditions disagree with a modern or majority consensus, the intentional aspects of the disagreement can be ignored as the conflictive aspects are reduced to different groups contesting their relative powers in the legal and/or political realms.

Ironically, while this has been the fate generally of religious discourse in our culture for some time, a complaint is now heard that it has become the fate of our political discourse. Issues are not intelligently and rationally debated: They are settled by courts or elections. Without genuine communicative praxis, the decisions of either are only dogmatically decisionistic. Social power, not understood as having its source in ongoing cooperative communication, is alienated into power to impose one's will upon others by the judicious use of manipulative cunning, whether in legal or political forums.[63]

---

[63] Lonergan, "Dialectic of Authority," 5–12. Also Matthew Lamb, "The Notion of the Transcultural in Bernard Lonergan's Theology," *Method: A Journal of Lonergan Studies* 8 (1990): 48–73.

If, as is said, languages are dialects with armies and navies, then, when the source of social power shifts from cooperation to manipulation, communicative consensus would be opinions with bank accounts and pressure groups. Understanding and reasons are not discussed but simply presumed to be associated with forceful and authoritarian groups. The public realm, as it excludes the dead, the poor, and the marginalized, loses its human orientation and becomes a battlefield of warring opinions and decisions. Dogmatic competition replaces communicative praxis.

Christian theologians whose theology is rooted in communities of orthopraxis will realize that "the weak messianic power of the present"[64] is informed with a grace and Spirit that transforms our weakness into the gentle strength and Presence of God. In the Risen Christ we are united into a communion of communities that embraces and transforms humankind, not through dominative force but through quiet faith, undying hope, and a love that all the hate and indifference in the world cannot extinguish. Christian theologies for the public realms communicate a universality through the solidarity of the reign of God *(basileia tou qeou)* that the whole Christ preaches and practices against the empires and superpowers down the ages.

---

64 Habermas, *The Philosophical Discourse of Modernity,* 14–15: "It is no longer only future generations, but past generations as well, that have a claim on the weak messianic power of the present. The anamnestic redemption of an injustice, which cannot of course be undone but can at least be virtually reconciled through remembering, ties up the present with the communicative context of a universal historical solidarity. This anamnesis constitutes the decentering counterpoise to the dangerous concentration of responsibility that modern time-consciousness, oriented exclusively toward the future, has laid on the shoulders of a problematic present that has, as it were, been tied in knots."

Index

About the Cover

Plaque with the Journey to Emmaus and the Noli Me Tangere.
ca. 1115–1120. Ivory, traces of gilding, $10\,5/8 \times 5\,5/16$ in. (27×13.5 cm).
Spanish, made in León. Gift of J. Pierpont Morgan, 1917 (17.190.47).
The Metropolitan Museum of Art, New York, NY, U.S.A.